Developing
New
Services

Developing New Services

Edited by:
William R. George
Villanova University

Claudia E. Marshall
Travelers Insurance Company

Proceedings Series

AMERICAN
MARKETING
A$SOCIATION   250 South Wacker Drive · Chicago, Illinois 60606 · 312/648-0536

©American Marketing Association

1984

Printed in the United States of America

Cover Design by Cory DeLacey

LIBRARY OF CONGRESS CATALOGING IN PUBCN. DATA

Main entry under title:
Developing new services.
  (Proceedings series/American Marketing Assn)
Proceedings of a conference held Oct. 17-18, 1983,
at Villanova University, Villanova, Pa.
  1. Service industries--Congresses. 2. Marketing--
Congresses. I. George, William R. II. Marshall,
Claudia E. III. Series.
HD9980.5.D48 1984   658.4'06   83-22668
ISBN 0-87757-165-1

This book was prepared from camera-ready copy supplied by
the authors. In case of a chart's illegibility, the reader
should contact the author of the specific article.

090/2000/484

TABLE OF CONTENTS

SYNOPSIS AND FOREWORD

This Proceedings contains the presentations of a Symposium on Developing New Services which was held at Villanova University on October 17-18, 1983. The Symposium was sponsored by the American Marketing Association and is the Association's third program focusing on the marketing of services. Once again, as with the two earlier programs, a special enthusiasm resulting from the collaborative efforts of services marketing practitioners and academics was evident. Attendance included 18 academics and 45 practitioners.

New services development has been recognized to be a topic of major importance to services marketers. For example, in a recent meeting of the steering committee on Services Marketing at the Marketing Science Institute, "new services development" was identified as number one out of ten topics to be considered as a research priority by the Institute.

The Symposium on Developing New Services focused on three basic themes:

1) developing a climate for innovation of new services;

2) new services development systems and processes;

3) the role of employees in new services development.

These themes merged to form an integrated focus on those elements critical to effective design and implementation of a new service. Key questions were raised. How are the human efforts of services workers involved in a new service affected by the culture of an organization? How can service design be influenced through both a supportive organization climate as well as a 'service ethic' among those employees who implement the new service? How can new services be systematically conceived and "blueprinted" to insure a detailed, consistent standard for service delivery? How much of what we know about product development of consumer goods is directly applicable to services?

A fundamental notion derived from the presentations and group discussions is the recognition of a difference in the development process for services as compared to goods. New services development involves a unique process of employee participation in both the early stages of ideation/conceptualization and in the implementation stage of the new services effort.

In exploring issues related to employee participation level, Stephen Zimney used the phrase "discretionary effort." The term describes the difference between the maximum amount of effort and care that a person can devote to the performance of his job in contrast to the minimum amount of effort the employee can exhibit to keep the job.

Ben Schneider and David Bowen in a similar manner contrast the "service ethic" to an "efficiency ethic." Goods manufacturers have been able to manage and control the efforts of the employee largely through the organization and structure of the assembly line itself. The innate structure and organization create an "efficiency ethic." However, for the service firm, a "service ethic," resulting from the maximum expenditure of human "discretionary" effort by employees, can create the distinguishing characteristic of the service which differentiates it from other competitive offerings. These elements are fundamental to the formation of the quality aspects of the service as perceived by the customer. Employee participation in the new service development process can lead to a cumulative definition of the service ethic and to increasing the discretionary effort of employees in performing their jobs.

The Symposium participants also concluded that managing cumulative discretionary efforts to create the service ethic in an organization is a very complex task because of the fundamental influence of an organization's corporate culture on its systems design processes. Lynn Shostack believes that the management of these complexities can be aided through a detailed service design process (blueprinting) which involves the three stages of analysis, synthesis and implementation. The blueprinting process assists service employees to effectively implement the new service because they can visualize its conceptualization and design before actual implementation. Thus during implementation, employees will consistently execute the service in a way that is discernible to customers. The complex task described here reinforces the importance of utilizing the management of a consistent corporate culture to communicate consistent cues to employees which further bond their unified efforts.

Corporate culture is a possible factor in the proposition of Schneider and Bowen that people use a certain degree of selectivity and empathy when choosing to work for a certain kind of organization. (We believe a further extension here may be that the customer uses a similar type of selectivity in choosing the type of organization which he wants to deal with.)

Schwartz suggests that "guiding beliefs" of a culture

outline the basic principles of the organization and should be
indicated through its mission and overall strategy. He believes that "daily beliefs" show how the guiding beliefs are
executed and demonstrated by the behaviors of the employees.
These two sets of organizational beliefs help to define the corporate culture and bond people together in the organization.
In essence, managing the corporate culture can ultimately influence management of the discretionary efforts of employees,
thus creating a service ethic. Thus the commitment of top
management to provide guiding beliefs and reinforce them
through the service innovation design and implementation process are critical factors for organizational success.

Patricia Meyers focused on success factors in product development by contrasting the differences between project teams
whose efforts resulted in successful or unsuccessful product
development results. The difference was not in the knowledge
or caliber of team members. Both project teams were staffed
with highly skilled people. The difference resulted from the
understanding by the team members of the context for its objectives. Specific requirements for success were a clear understanding of corporate goals, the presence of a facilitating
structure, an awareness of competition and an understanding of
marketing and customer needs. Those teams who were successful
clearly understood the context of their role and their importance in their organization at large. They understood the organization's culture and mission and understood their task
within the broad spectrum of customer markets being served by
the corporation.

Underscoring the management of a successful innovative
climate is a belief system that emphasizes and reinforces the
need to learn, rather than to record and "bean count" successes
and failures. This commentary takes us back full circle to the
notion of discretionary effort and the choices that individual
employees make, whether sublimally or directly, to participate
to their fullest capacities to the task at hand. The services
company facing new service development needs to respond to
these challenges:

1) understanding both the management of the collective
    efforts of human beings through the creation of a
    "service ethic" in the guiding principles of an or-
    ganization's culture; and

2) blueprinting the specific complexities of the in-
    dividual new service and its delivery to maximize
    employee understanding and commitment to the de-
    tails of service delivery at every stage of the
    new service development process.

The three components for successful development of new services are climate, detailed mapping and employees motivated by a service ethic.

The eight presenters did an outstanding job of analyzing new service development, each from their own special perspectives. The results were an obvious synergy that provides a unique compendium on this important topic. These presenters include:

David Bowen, University of Southern California;

Glendon E. French, ARA Health Care Sector, Philadelphia (luncheon speaker);

Christopher Lovelock, Harvard University;

Patricia Meyers, University of Massachusetts, Amherst;

Benjamin Schneider, University of Maryland;

Howard Schwartz, Management Analysis Center, Cambridge, MA;

G. Lynn Shostack, Bankers Trust; and

Stephen Zimney, Yankelovich, Skelly & White.

Each of the attendees selected one of three theme areas to examine in a small discussion group. Group facilitators reported back to the entire audience on these three-hour discussion group sessions the next morning. Edited participant perspectives appear at the end of each of the three sections of this Proceedings. The task of synthesizing these discussions was very ably handled by the following facilitators:

Bernard H. Booms, Washington State University, Seattle Center;

C. Robert Clements, University of Massachusetts-Boston Harbor Campus;

John A. Czepiel, New York University;

Duane Davis, University of Central Florida;

Dennis Guseman, University of Northern Colorado;

Nancy Hansen, University of New Hampshire;

Ronald Stiff, University of Baltimore; and

Valarie A. Zeithaml, Texas A & M University.

Two speakers gave closing remarks on future directions for services marketing. They were Leonard L. Berry, Texas

A & M University and chairman of the Services Marketing Planning Committee, American Marketing Association; and Diane H. Schmalensee, Marketing Science Institute. Clearly, many challenges and opportunities exist in all areas of services marketing research and applications.

We believe that the Symposium and Proceedings provide another large piece to the services marketing puzzle. It was a stimulating and rewarding experience to organize and conduct this event. We look forward to participating in future assemblies that explore other aspects of services marketing.

William R. George   Claudia E. Marshall
Villanova University   The Travelers Companies
Villanova, PA   19085   Hartford, CT   06115

DEVELOPING A CLIMATE FOR INNOVATION OF NEW SERVICES

Howard Schwartz, Management Analysis Center

I want to talk about the role that corporate culture plays
in creating the kinds of conditions in which change and innovation can take place. Management Analysis Center has in the last
five years increasingly focused on the problems large organizations have in implementing major strategic change. I want to
share with you some prospectives based on work with senior management groups in a number of large organizations.

Business Week (October 27, 1980) did a cover story on corporate culture that asked "How do we understand the hard-to-
change values that cause success or failure." That article was
originated by a contact we had with Business Week concerning
the notion of corporate culture. We think it explains a lot
about the difficulties that companies have making major strategic change. Most recently, the current edition of Fortune
(October 12, 1983) has a cover story that draws largely on the
work that we at Management Analysis Center have been doing, particularly in the last three years. Why all this interest in
the topic of corporate culture? I think the interest comes
from two sources. First, the ability of organizations to make
organizational change is a key strategic variable, a major factor in their ability to compete. The kind of trends and changes
that technology and deregulation have had (e.g. on the banking
industry and financial services more broadly) has been profound.
The need to manage knowledge workers in the services industries
is causing organizations to have to change the way they operate.
If you think about the kind of massive change that is involved
in restructuring the delivery systems in a consumer banking
business and restructuring what people do within those delivery
systems and in building and integrating the kind of electronic
information networks that are necessary to run those businesses
today, you begin to see the dimensions of change that companies
are increasingly facing. Second, I think one can say that the
70's for many companies was the age of marketing. In the 70's
many companies discovered the niches that were out there. I
think one might accurately say that the 80's for most companies
must be the age of innovation. A firm must determine how to
serve those niches more effectively than the competition if it
is going to have above average returns. Organizational effectiveness is becoming a key strategic weapon and that is particularly true about service businesses.

I would like to focus on the topic of corporate culture,
particularly from a top management perspective, and on the im-

1

pact culture has on the ability of organizations to manage increased rates of innovation and change. What is corporate culture and where does it come from? I think you can argue that corporate culture is a set of patterns, beliefs, and values that are deeply held, often historically developed -- a transfer from one generation to another in the organization. Marvin Bower in his book, The Will to Manage, said that corporate culture is "the way we do things around here." It affects the way we compete and the way we manage. Several examples can illustrate this. For those of you who know Morgan Guaranty, Morgan sees itself as a bank. Morgan does not want to be a financial services conglomerate and it is a deeply held value at Morgan that effects everything that they do. Many observers of General Electric say that G.E. always approaches markets and competitors the same way and if you understand it, you can predict what they are going to do.

I recently talked with a major food company that said: "We want to codify how we manage -- what is it we do about the way we manage that makes for success. We think we understand it but we do not know how to articulate it and we want to really capture that aspect of what we do." These are reflections of the fact that organizations have corporate cultures. Those cultures are subject, over a period of time, to managerial action. You can manage them within limits. If the cultural beliefs are strongly held and inappropriate to what you are trying to do with the business, you better understand it. And, if cultural beliefs are not deeply felt and widely shared across your organization, that is going to cost plenty in terms of the ability to coordinate and integrate across organizational lines.

A discussion of culture should start with the question of where it comes from. I find it useful to think in terms of four driving forces that shape the culture of the organization. One of the problems with a lot of the work that is done in this field is that people tend to only look at the first and the third as being the primary drivers of where culture comes from in the organization. First, history is important. Every organization goes through a series of experiences from which important lessons have been learned. Those lessons become the conventional wisdom. Second, I think not enough attention is given to the fact that the culture of any organization is shaped a lot by the critical success factors in its industry. Third, the values and beliefs of the top leadership, particularly if there was a strong founder, are significant. A final factor, which too often is under-estimated, is the impact that the structure, measurement and management process have in shaping and maintaining the organization's culture.

2

Kodak, for example, has a history of innovation. But it is highly centralized innovation, taking place in a very few areas of the firm. The critical success factors in that business have involved scale and the maintenance of patent protection over an extended period of time. Kodak is essentially a functional organization with a top leadership that values highly centralized decision making and a set of structured management processes that are very functional in focus. Banks provide another example. Their profit model is shifting from financial intermediation to information systems management. When you see the profit model changing in an industry, that is a clear sign that the industry is going to be undergoing severe cultural change.

When thinking about corporate cultures, it is very useful to divide culture into two basic notions. We call these two notions guiding beliefs and daily beliefs. The set of guiding beliefs are fundamental while the daily beliefs shape the things done within that overall context. Companies have such beliefs and those beliefs powerfully shape the decisions and daily actions that get made and effect their ability to change and to innovate. (We need to put culture in some perspective. I think it is an error to argue that culture is the only thing that matters in an organization. Culture is one of four aspects of an organization -- structure, systems, people and culture). The guiding beliefs precede the strategy. For example, there are fundamental assumptions about life such as IBM's basic assumption that it is going to offer the best customer service in the world. Another one of its fundamental basic beliefs is respect for the individual. Out of those two basic beliefs at IBM much strategy, much direction and much policy and procedure ultimately emanates. The daily beliefs of an organization interact with the other elements to shape what happens every day. They have a great deal to do with the ability to implement and execute the choices that are made about strategic direction. However, one never wants the daily beliefs to shape strategic choice. That is the tail wagging the dog. Yet in those companies that do not have a clear, well understood set of guiding beliefs that are shared across the organization, that is almost always what happens. The lack of a clear set of guiding beliefs that are appropriate to a changing environment is one of the principle reasons organizations have difficulty in coping with change.

Let us consider some guiding beliefs across a number of dimensions that affect the life of an organization. These beliefs are derived from a number of companies. The framework used in helping organizations to think about their guiding beliefs involves an analysis of their history and an understanding of their generic activities like strategy, marketing, tech-

3

nology, people and organization. We develop with the senior management group the recognition of how these ideas shape strategic choice and how they determine the way the organization is managed.

Guiding beliefs about STRATEGY. Below are two statements of beliefs that were developed through a series of interviews in two different organizations. They were fed back to the senior management group and discussed until there was some agreement that they in fact did capture the essence of how the organization felt about strategy, not its contents but its beliefs about strategy as a first principle.

Company A Strategy Statement: From your actions, define the business your competitors will follow you in (and communicate it to your employees so that their daily behavior reinforces the intention). In this organization the strategy must be passed along in the language of action, not the language of words. Behavior, not articulation, is important here. Strategy is being used as a tool to get entrepreneurial risk taking. To do this, strategy must be used more as a communicator than as a message to be communicated. This company believes that strategy has to be shared with the organization to make a difference.

Company A's approach is a profound change from the way most organizations look at strategy. Note that strategy formulation started in capital intensive organizations where the ability to make a small number of very important decisions about where the organization is going to invest its dollars and the timing of these investments is what matters. Here one can drive strategy into the firm from the top. Secrecy to keep the competition from knowing where, when and how large of an investment was justified.

However, in service organizations and multi-product, multi-market firms, such secrecy is the wrong approach since it means that people close to the business do not get involved in developing the strategy. Secrecy means they do not know what the strategy is and when it is finally communicated to them, they do not feel any ownership or participation in it. This belief about a service firm's strategy argues that even your customers ought to know what your strategy is. For example, a number of years ago when Citibank was in the middle of making some major commitments, their view was that they wanted everyone to know what they were doing including competitors. Their belief was that they were trying to make themselves so different from most of their competitors that even if the competitors knew, they could not respond effectively to the strategy.

4

Company B's Strategy Statement: In uncertain environments, emphasize flexibility and selective strategic positioning. This company was very slow to get innovation off the ground. They were involved in lots of small experiments, but no big bets. They were always playing catch-up, with very centralized decision making. Nobody knew what the strategy was.

Clearly, if a company understands what its fundamental belief is about strategy, that begins to explain the kinds of choices it makes and its ability to execute them.

Guiding beliefs about MARKETING. Peter Drucker said years ago that marketing is so basic that it cannot be considered a separate function: it is the whole business seen from the point of view of its final result, i.e., from the customer's point of view. Below are top management beliefs about marketing in two companies.

Company C Marketing Statement: Use marketing as a tool for differentiating customers, and determining how we can serve them profitably. Here marketing is a closely held tool only understood by a few. The marketing function was resisted by the line organization. There was no user demand for the services supplied. In fact, one can see in the statement that what this company was trying to do was to meet its own needs for profitability rather than the needs of its customers.

Company D Marketing Statement: Provide what customers need, where and when they want it, at a profit. Here marketing really was a way of life and Drucker's maxim did apply. Company C was a lagging follower; Company D is a highly profitable, very successful innovator.

Guiding beliefs about TECHNOLOGY. Beliefs about technology in financial services, and particularly beliefs about risk taking with respect to technology, are going to be one of the things that separates the winners from the losers in that industry. These beliefs are going to shape the directions in which a lot of the big financial institutions are going. Two financial institutions illustrate this.

Company E Technology Statement: Invest so intensively in scale economic technologies as to drive out competition.

Company F Technology Statement: Lead in implementation of proven technologies, to attain scale economies present in an electronic future. Both banks perceive technology as a strategic weapon, but in fact would go in very different directions in terms of the aggressiveness with which they were prepared to use technology. Company E's approach to managing technology utilizes a more decentralized management structure with much tighter linkages between the marketing units and the managers of technology. There was much innovation and successful use of technology here. Company F had a highly centralized technical organization with many delays and disagreements about where they ought to invest. There was a lack of market drivenness. The beliefs of these two financial organizations resulted in vastly different approaches to technology.

Guiding beliefs about IMPLEMENTATION. Implementation is used here as a catch all phrase to summarize other important belief areas within the organization. Two contrasting beliefs illustrate a 'do-it-fix-it' organization vs. a 'study-it-test-it' organization.

Company G Statement: Prefer the dramatically pre-emptive to the dependably executed.

Company H Statement: First in service means dependable execution. Company G sees itself as wanting to act now and willing to take some short term costs of poor service to customers in order to be a leader and to learn from experience. Company H, on the other hand, is never a leader, never an innovator. For example, Proctor and Gamble is a company that many of us think of as a highly innovative organization, certainly a very successful product developer. But I would argue that recent articles about P&G suggest that it is trying to change itself at least to some extent from an 'H-type' company to a 'G-type' company. Apparently P&G realizes that the bureaucratic controls that are involved with its "study-and-test-it" philosophy have begun to cause it to lag behind in quite a number of product categories. Implementing that kind of shift is a major undertaking.

Where do we go from here? Shifting guiding beliefs is very difficult to do. When management begins to understand what its guiding beliefs are, they need to ask themselves: "Is this the kind of an organization that we want to be? Do we need to be innovative? Do the beliefs that drive our company allow us to be as innovative as we need to be in this business, given the way it is changing? What kind of a company can we be if these are our guiding beliefs?" If management does not like its current culture, it is a big job to change guiding beliefs. If an organization does not have consensus, clarity and commitment to guiding beliefs, "the tail will wag the dog." That is, daily beliefs in the organization will end up determining priorities for action. This will limit the ability of Senior Management to execute it's desired course of action.

6

We may ask why some of the more obvious techniques that companies use to foster innovation often fail to have the kind of impact that is sought. For example, hiring more innovative people who just somehow do not seem to be able to work in the organization. Or smaller organizational units with better delegation to task teams that just do not seem to get the job done. Or product champions who blunt their sword. Or venture funding is used as a means of getting around some of these problems. Yet when the venture managers are interviewed, they all report they are going to quit the company because what really matters in getting ahead in the organization is making your numbers. And venture managers almost by definition are not going to make their numbers. Often the attempts to move away from the focus on short term performance end up being little more than lip service. These changes are so difficult to achieve because in many cases the daily beliefs in the organization will frustrate the intent of these kinds of organizational approaches to achieve higher rates of innovation.

We use a framework to help a company understand what their daily beliefs are. It is a corporate culture matrix which includes a set of tasks that are defined in terms relevant to the particular organization (e.g., innovating, decision-making, communicating, organization, monitoring, and appraising/rewarding) and a set of relationships (e.g., company-wide, boss-subordinate, peer, inter-department). What must be done is to understand the daily beliefs that shape the way in which those relationship tasks get managed. For the financial institutions discussed earlier, peer relationships can be summarized as: information is power, guard it; be a gentleman, don't confront; etc., while relationships between departments in these organizations tend to be driven by notions that say protect your P & L, form alliances but only around specific issues and guard your turf carefully. Once you begin to understand the way these daily beliefs work, they tell you how they might frustrate some of those specific measures that one might choose to put in place to try to make some innovation happen.

The corporate culture matrix tells executives that we should consider the use of techniques and approaches like task teams or new information systems in light of compatibility with the daily beliefs of the culture that is in place. At this point we can begin to pinpoint where our problems are and make some systematic assessments about where we should place some management attention. These ideas are developed in considerable detail in Schwartz and Davis', "Matching Corporate Culture and Business."

In summary, the CEO contemplating cultural change must

have an agenda which includes the following: develop a shared business vision; determine desired change in behavior and values; set change strategy -- pace, timing, cost; use the CEO office to lead; reorient power to support new values; and harness high-impact systems and operating mechanisms. At General Electric, for example, this involves changing the reward system, the resource allocation process, and the appointments process.

Five steps are recommended for 'How to Proceed' in initiating a culture change: 1. Get awareness and agreement about the culture and its impact; 2. Define the relevant culture and subcultures in your organization; 3. Organize statements about your firm's culture in terms of guiding beliefs and daily beliefs; 4. Assess the risks your company's culture presents for the formulation and implementation of strategic change; and, 5. Develop an action plan to manage culture risk.

REFERENCE

Schwarz, Howard and S. M. Davis (1981), "Matching Corporate Culture and Business Strategy," Organizational Dynamics (Summer) 30-48.

INNOVATION SHIFT: LESSONS FOR SERVICE FIRMS FROM A TECHNOLOGICAL LEADER

Patricia W. Meyers, University of Massachusetts, Amherst

ABSTRACT

This paper puts forward some propositions about the nature of a shift toward innovation in a high technology business and about the organizational conditions that characterize successful shift toward higher order innovations. Results of an exploratory study of changes in the innovation management process in a leading office products firm are discussed. These, coupled with lessons learned from other studies of high technology innovation, form the basis for suggested means to encourage the innovation process in service firms.

INTRODUCTION

The research, development, and launch of new products and innovations has been a well-researched area in marketing for some time (Crawford 1983; Pessimier 1977; Rothberg 1981; Urban and Hauser 1980). Likewise, the development of new technologies and the so-called "high" (meaning "advanced") technology products which often follow (e.g., the development of microprocessors and the numerous new products and features they make possible) has also been a subject of active investigation (Abernathy 1978; Cooper 1979, 1980; Rothwell 1972; Utterback 1974). In contrast, the development and diffusion of innovative services has received attention only recently and from comparatively few authors (Robinson 1983; Shostack 1981). While a significant body of research on the service innovation process is yet to accumulate, it is possible to begin bridging this knowledge gap by extrapolating carefully from existing knowledge about the development of some discriminatingly chosen product innovations. The rationale for such a comparison and extrapolation is based on the heavy service component that must be included in any product innovation that requires perceptual or behavioral change on the part of the potential user.

Levitt (1972, p. 42) has pointed out that "there are no such things as service industries . . . only industries whose service components are greater or less than those of other industries." We can accept Levitt's notion that to some degree "everybody is in service." Add to this the lessons of diffusion theory that higher order innovations are adopted most rapidly when their intangible characteristics are dealt with

9

effectively by the change agent from the user's standpoint.
These intangible characteristics include Rogers' (1968) well-
known charateristics of innovations: for example, potential
adopters' perceptions of the new offering in terms of compatibility with existing values and norms, risk of trial, relative
advantage and so forth. Thus, technological innovations that
require attitudinal, perceptual, or behavioral change in the
user have heavy intangible components just as services do. It
follows that investigation of innovation processes in high
technology products may well yield some organizational lessons
for innovative services development and marketing.

Innovation Defined.
     One recurring difficulty when considering innovation of any
type is definition. Like the apple pie and motherhood of by-
gone eras, innovation today--especially technological innova-
tion--is a concept about which almost everyone feels positively,
but which also raises expectations, dreams, doubts, and reser-
vations. One finds it hard to discuss innovation without
tapping some strongly felt, highly charged personal values
structure ranging over such diverse topics as national economic
renewal, Japanese managerial techniques, personal creativity,
self-actualization, entrepreneurship, and structural unemployment. It would help ground this investigation, therefore, to
define innovation as it is applied here. Based upon the previous discussions of several scholars on the various meanings
of "innovation" in business and related disciplines (Tinnesand
1973; Mansfield 1971; Schumpeter 1950), we can consider business innovation to be the ability of an organization to match
technological discovery (heretofore unapplied technology or
technology that is now to be applied in a new way) with market
discoveries (whether new user segments, new distribution
methods, or new pricing approaches) to produce a profit.

     Several types of innovation exist and taxonomies have been
proposed (Robertson 1971; Zaltman, Duncan, and Holbek 1973).
Figure 1 depicts a useful conceptualization that incorporates
the several approaches. Innovations may be sorted along two
dimensions: (1) degree of perceptual and/or behavioral change
needed to adopt on the part of the potential user, and (2) degree of technological newness to the firm. Combinations of low
or high degrees along these two dimensions produce four cells
filled by tertiary, secondary, or primary innovation types.

     Tertiary innovations (cell 1) include style changes, fami-
liar add-ons and me-too products and services. These altered
offerings require little change in potential user perceptions
or behaviors. They seldom involve technologies that are unfamiliar to the firm. These are the least risky innovations, but
often offer the lowest pay back over the long term.

10

FIGURE 1

Degree of User
Perceptual/Behavioral Change
Needed to Adopt

		Low	High
Degree of Technological	Low	1. Tertiary Innovation	2. Secondary Innovation
Newness to the Firm	High	3. Secondary Innovation	4. Primary Innovation

Examples of secondary innovations (cells 2 and 3) include such offerings as programmable calculators, telephone calling cards, or self-written airline tickets. Such innovations involve some degree of user perceptual and behavioral change but do not involve extremely different use patterns. They may require some technology that is new to the firm, but the base knowledge usually exists within the organization. Both the risk level and the long-term pay back of secondary innovations are in the mid-range.

Finally, primary innovations (cell 4), such as the first commercially available telephones, automobiles, and personal computers, require and stimulate markedly different perceptions and behaviors in users. Most often, primary innovations involve technological knowledge that is new to the firm. Indeed, frequently this knowledge arises outside the industry of the firm. These are the most risky innovations for firms; but when successful, they provide high returns over the long run.

It is the needed perceptual and behavioral alteration in users in both secondary and primary innovations that require careful management of the intangible aspects of the innovation. Here the lessons of product innovation and service marketing dovetail since, by definition, services are distinguished by their relatively high intangibility (Berry 1980; Levitt 1981; Shostak 1977).

Innovation Shift
The histories of several technologically-based firms reveal a cycling innovation pattern over time in which any one firm moves through periods of high innovation, transitions, and relatively low innovation (Abernathy 1978; Schon 1967, 1971). Using the terminology presented here, a technological firm

often begins around a primary innovation, such as the automobile, moves into secondary innovations that modify the original innovation, and then reach a relatively stable plateau in which tertiary innovations predominate. Certain environmental changes, most frequently the entry of effective competitors with rival offerings, can stimulate the firm to seek new secondary or even primary innovations to regain or hold profitability and position (Klein 1979). This move toward higher order innovation and the organizational process whereby it is successfully managed is termed here the innovation shift.

The case comparison which follows is an exploratory study of this innovation shift in a leading high technology firm. It is proposed that aspects of this process may take place in service firms as well. This occurrence would seem most probable where service industries appear to be involved in an innovation shift toward higher levels of innovative activity. Banking and television broadcasting, for example, appear to be moving from formerly stable, tertiary innovation production and consumption patterns to a more unstable secondary or even primary innovation production and consumption stage.

The following sections describe the methodology and findings of an exploratory case comparison study of the innovation shift process in one Fortune 500 firm, propose implications for the findings for service firms, and suggest areas for much needed further research.

METHODOLOGY

Public statements of senior managers of an acknowledged technological leader in the office products industry indicated a corporate decision to shift a major division of the firm from relatively stable, teriary innovations to higher order innovations. Preliminary interviews with 18 top managers in 6 functional areas (2 or 3 in each function) confirmed this commitment. Using a multiple method approach (interviews, nonparticipant observation, archival data, and a survey instrument), the researcher was able to identify and examine two new product development and launch team efforts that occurred after the corporate decision to increase innovation level along the dimensions of new technologies and perceptual/behavioral change in users.

Unit of Analysis
The new product project team is charged with "marrying" the technology of the R&D function with the knowledge of the user for which the marketing function is responsible. It would follow that, in firms producing advanced technological products,

12

the locus of much active innovation process activity would occur where individual business functions, such as R&D and marketing, must be joined to make and launch a new product, that is, in the new product project team. This is not to say that the innovative process does not take place in other organizational groups. It is reasonable, however, that the project team is, by nature of its charter, focused on producing innovation as we have defined it. This high degree of focus makes the project team a suitable research site for viewing the process of innovation shift.

Case Study Comparison

Two project teams utilizing similar technologies to produce their separate products were located in the same division. One project followed the other in time. This condition was essential to an investigation of any changes in innovative process over time. Both projects were to produce products that were judged by company managers to require moderate behavior changes in the way potential buyers would use the product. As such, they dealt with secondary innovations.

Project Alpha. The first of the projects, Alpha, took three years in the development and launch stages. The resulting product, a secondary innovation which incorporated some innovative combinations of features, was recalled for extensive redesign shortly after national launch. Under these conditions it could be considered an unsuccessful innovation, since it did not produce a profit in the marketplace.

Project Beta. The development and launch phases of Beta followed in time shortly after Alpha's recall. Beta also took three years to develop, and was launched nationally in 1982. Market response has been very enthusiastic, with initial orders running far ahead of available supply. Beta enjoyed more corporate resources than Alpha, primarily because it was a larger project in scope. (Alpha's team included nearly 400 people, where Beta's was almost 2000 strong at its height.) The projects were comparable, however, in several important dimensions. Both groups suffered resource restriction at various stages in the development cycle. With one exception, core team managers on both projects had 9 or more years experience with the company and the core technology. All but one had worked on previous new product introductions. Thus, the core team managers were almost equally experienced. In addition, technologies used in both projects were known but were combined in new and different ways.

Design and Data Collection. Within the multi-method case study approach, the design consisted of in-depth interviews and a survey of the project manager and of the four key

13

functional managers directly under him on each project: engineering, manufacturing, marketing, and planning. Survey instrument questions focused on 9 project/new product success variables discussed in the next section. Open-ended questions concentrated on differences between the two projects. In all, 10 managers were interviewed for an average of two hours each. Most were interviewed more than once. In addition, the division head was also interviewed. Conclusions were reviewed with with the project manager and two of the key managers (one from each project) and with two vice presidents outside the projects as a check on internal validity.

Variables and Hypotheses. The survey phase of the case comparison selected 9 variables that previous studies found to be associated with project team/new product success. These variables, which were measured using multiple questions in the survey, included the following: clarity of corporate goals (Materna 1981); a facilitating organizational structure (Souder 1983); awareness of competition (Calantone and Cooper 1981); commitment to marketing knowledge and practice (Rothwell 1972); overall project management effectiveness (Rubenstein et al. 1976); clarity of individual tasks and roles (Frohman 1978); ease of information flow (Tushman 1979); resolution of technical problems (Myers and Marquis 1969) and resolution of manufacturing problems (Abernathy and Utterback 1979). In view of the small sample size (n=10), responses on Likert-type, 5-point scales were collected in two-by-two tables by positive and not positive answer categories and compared between teams using the appropriate non-parametric statistical technique. Summary tables with Fisher exact test results are at the Appendix.

It was hypothesized that the key managers of the successful team, Beta, would perceive the project to be more positive on all 9 variables. Thus, the null hypothesis for each variable was one of no difference. The alternative hypothesis for each variable was that Project Beta, the successful innovation, would be perceived more positively on each of the variables commonly associated with successful innovation process.

Analysis of responses to the open-ended questions that were related to the 9 variables were examined. Responses about perceived procedural and process differences between the two projects were analyzed.

14

FINDINGS

Process Comparison Between Projects Alpha and Beta

Similarities. The perception of key team managers on
both projects showed no statistical differences and were qualitatively similar on 5 of the 9 measured variables as follows:
  (1) Effectiveness of project management--Managers on
      both projects felt management had been largely
      effective.
  (2) Clarity of individual tasks and roles--On both teams
      managers felt their own tasks and own roles had been
      clear and unambiguous.
  (3) Easy information flow--All but one respondent felt
      information flowed easily and that it was okay to be
      open about problems.
  (4) Resolved technical problems--While technical problems
      were perceived as one barrier to success, learning
      in technical areas was perceived to be high on both
      projects.
  (5) Resolved manufacturing problems--While manufacturing
      problems were perceived as one barrier to success,
      learning in manufacturing areas was perceived to be
      high on both projects.

Differences. The perceptions of key team managers were
statistically different and qualitatively dissimilar by project on 4 of the 9 variables as follows:
  (1) Clarity of top management and corporate goals--As
      hypothesized, managers of the successful team per-
      ceived corporate goals to be clearer and more con-
      sistent.
  (2) A facilitating organizational structure--As hypothe-
      sized, managers on the successful team perceived
      organizational structure to be less of a barrier to
      their tasks than did managers on the unsuccessful
      project.
  (3) Awareness of competition--As hypothesized, managers
      of the successful team perceived more awareness of
      competitive moves in their decisions.
  (4) Commitment to marketing knowledge--As hypothesized,
      managers on the successful project perceived more
      commitment to obtaining and using information about
      market conditions and users.

The following interview data summaries concerning these
four statistically significant perceived differences between
the two projects will help to highlight important factors
underlying these differences. Corporate goals in Alpha were
perceived to be fairly clear at any given point. The relative

15

importance of these goals and the set of relevant goals were both perceived to have changed frequently during the course of the project, however. By contrast, corporate goals for the successful project, Beta, were not only perceived as clear but also as consistent over time. Goals were broadly stated so that implementation activities could be modified to meet unexpected conditions. But the desirable finishing points (e.g., quality product, lower unit manufacturing cost, customer satisfaction) remained stable and were clearly understood throughout the project. <u>Organizational structure</u> was changed in the middle of the unsuccessful project, Alpha, from a mixed matrix and functional approach to a full-blown matrix system across all functions. Alpha managers reported the matrix idea was felt to be sound in theory, but that its timing and implementation were confusing and frustrating--even counterproductive. This was especially true where matrix decision making processes suddenly made resource allocation a consensual process. For example, before the comprehensive matrix system, some technical managers had final say (within a comparatively broad range of availability) over resource allocation for their sub-teams. After the implementation of the matrix these managers had to convince line managers at a peer level that they should allocate resources to Alpha. The pioneering and cultivation needed for persuasion and consensual resource allocation took far more time than former decision making techniques. The necessary groundwork had not been laid, and, in some cases, managers lacked the experience needed to operate effectively in the new system. <u>Competitive awareness</u> was made an integral part of Beta's decision and tracking processes in the form of "competitive benchmarks." These frequently and regularly measured indicators provided readings on critical factors of competitive products (e.g., cost, price, service, performance quality, etc.) that were then used as targets for the development team to beat. In Alpha, information about new features on competitive products often surfaced after designs had been developed and locked into product architecture. This meant choosing between losing time redesigning product features or adding different features to offset a competitive disadvantage. <u>Commitment to marketing knowledge</u> in Beta was reported to be much more aggressively sought, more frequently used, and more flexibly applied than in Alpha. Alpha managers reported feeling that "no one knew the market as well as we did." Apparently this feeling was pervasive enough to blur negative signals from user tests early in the launch of Alpha's product. Data from these tests eventually caused product withdrawal after national announcement and launch. Ideally, however, these data should have served as early warnings to delay launch altogether. Project Beta did employ early and aggressive user test to iron out product design, manufacturing, and installation wrinkles so as to assure quality performance before national launch. In addition, Beta enjoyed more flexibility in traditional marketing mix elements such as distribution mechanisms and pricing structure. Finally, and perhaps most importantly from the standpoint of service firms, the single most frequently mentioned change from Alpha to Beta was the need for increased commitment to the service components of the high technology new product. Logically, the market launch of a tertiary innovation does not require unusual or extensive service to the user beyond that which is already functioning. Indeed, if the consumption patterns for the product class are well established, the firm producing tertiary innovations may cut back or standardize services to lower costs. The introduction of secondary or primary innovations, with the new consumption patterns they demand of the user, require increased, often tailor-made support service to the user. These to help overcome reluctance adopt the new product.

Thus, both survey and interview data in the case comparison indicate that for the time period identified as an innovation shift in one leading technological firm the following factors appear to have been most important to increasing effective innovative ability in new product project teams:

(1) The use of clear, communicable, and consistent corporate goals for the product. If stated broadly enough, these goals can guide the frequent changes in sub-goals and implementation activities that often accompany the development of secondary and primary innovation.

(2) The use of a flexible organizational structure which managers are trained to operate for the benefit of the new product.

(3) The frequent and regular monitoring of competitive moves along with a process that allows anticipating as well a responding to these quickly.

(4) The early implementation of mechanisms (such as user tests and personalized service) to foster new perceptual, attitudinal, and behavioral patterns in the potential adopter of the innovation.

DISCUSSION

While the results of a single case comparison are not broadly generalizable, the conclusions presented do offer some interesting perspectives for comparison with other studies and for future research. As already pointed out, past research has found that clear and consistent goals, flexible organizational structures, proactive attention to competitive moves, and continuing efforts to understand and meet user needs are among the most critical factors in successful innovation. What

17

the present study raises is the possibility that these four factors are most important in the process of innovation shift. That is, when a company moves from the production of tertiary innovations to that of secondary or primary innovations, these four factors may deserve the closest managerial attention and have the strongest claim for resource allocation among many competing factors because of the role that may play in successfully shifting a company toward higher order innovations.

Further research is needed to decide conclusively whether these four factors are particular to the circumstances of this one firm or industry. As noted earlier, however, several technology-based American firms (such as Polaroid in cameras, Ford in autos, Texas Instruments in personal computers) do appear to have similar problems in making the innovative shift and these problems do appear to reside, at least in part, with the four factors that emerged in the current study.

LESSONS FOR INNOVATION IN SERVICE COMPANIES

For service companies that have been most recently involved in tertiary innovations (or even more stable offerings), we can make some interesting speculations about ways to increase successful innovative capability. (No claim can be made to presenting authoritative strictures for increasing successful innovation process within the confines of the current study, but some points for discussion and some hints about proper directions are in order.)

Service companies may benefit from considering the following in their efforts to shift to higher order innovative activity:

(1) judicious use of new service project teams to integrate functional areas such as marketing and operations during the development and launch of new services

(2) phased implementation of flexible organizational structures, such as matrix and strategic business unit systems to facilitate project team activity

(3) active training of new service project managers in the effective operation of flexible organization structures in ways that maximize team effectiveness in carrying out their tasks

(4) sustained attention to planned systems that monitor competitive firms and of anticipating their likely innovation stance

(5) creative design of service-specific new offering test activities that perform functions similar to new product user tests

18

(6) early organizational commitment to supporting secondary and primary innovation adoption with complementary services and marketing techniques (such as user
education and tailor-made support to lead users).

Despite the many differences between service- and pro-
duct-dominant organizations, several basic characteristics of
higher order innovations may be comparable between them.
Lessons learned in product innovation research should be helpful to improve innovation processes in our most rapidly expanding business sector--services. The foregoing study suggests some preliminary ways to begin this important transfer
of knowledge.

APPENDIX

POOLED CASE COMPARISON DATA TABLES AND
FISHER EXACT TEST RESULTS

Variable 1: Clear Corporate Goals

Alpha	Beta	
5	13	Positive Response
10	2	Non-Positive Response

n=30; p=.004

Variable 2: Facilitating Structure

Alpha	Beta	
2	7	Pos
8	3	Non-Pos

n=20; p=.035

Variable 3: Awareness of Competition

Alpha	Beta	
4	10	Pos
6	0	Non-Pos

n=20; p=.005

Variable 4: Marketing

Alpha	Beta	
2	8	Pos
8	2	Non-Pos

n=20; p=.012

Variable 5: Project Management Issues

Alpha	Beta	
9	12	Pos
6	3	Non-Pos

n=30; p=.213

Variable 6: Clarity of Own Tasks and Roles

Alpha	Beta	
9	9	Pos
1	1	Non-Pos

n=20; p=1

Variable 7: Easy Information Flow

Alpha	Beta	
9	9	Pos
1	1	Non-Pos

n=20; p=1

Variable 8: Few Unaddressed Technical Problems

Alpha	Beta	
3	5	Pos
7	5	Non-Pos

n=20; p=.314

Variable 9: Few Unaddressed Manufacturing Problems

Alpha	Beta	
7	9	Pos
8	6	Non-Pos

n=30; p=.358

BIBLIOGRAPHY

Abernathy, William J. (1978), The Productivity Dilemma, Balti-
more: The Johns Hopkins Press.
_____ and James M. Utterback (1978), "Patterns of Industrial
Innovation," Technology Review, 80 (June/July), 41-47.
Berry, Leonard L. (1980), "Services Marketing Is Different,"
Business (May/June), 24-29.
Calantone, Roger and Robert G. Cooper (1981), "New Product
Scenarios: Prospects for Success," Journal of Marketing 45
(Spring), 48-60.
Cooper, Robert G. (1980), Project Newprod: What Makes a New
Product a Winner? Montreal: Quebec Industrial Innovation
Center.
_____ (1979), "The Dimensions of Industrial New Product Suc-
cess and Failure," Journal of Marketing 43 (Summer), 93-103.
Crawford, C. Merle (1983), New Products Management, Homewood,
Ill: Richard D. Irwin, Inc.
Frohman, Alan L. (1978), "The Performance of Innovation: Mana-
gerial Roles," California Management Review 20 (Spring), 5-
12.
Klein, Burton H. (1979), "The Slowdown in Productivity Ad-
vances," in Technological Innovation for A Dynamic Economy,
Christopher T. Hill and James M. Utterback, eds., New York:
Pergamon Press, 66-117.
Levitt, Theodore (1981), "Marketing Intangible Products and
Product Intangibles," Harvard Business Review (May-June),
94-102.
_____ (1972), "Production-line Approach to Service," Harvard
Business Review (September-October), 41-52.
Mansfield, Edwin (1971), Technological Change, New York: W.W.
Norton & Company, Inc.
Materna, Anthony T. (1981), "Study of Management Factors
Affecting Innovation Diffusion in High Technology," Unpub-
lished PhD dissertation, Claremont Graduate School.
Myers, Sumner and D. G. Marquis (1969), Successful Industrial
Innovations, Washington D.C.: National Science Foundation,
NSF 69-17.
Pessemier, Edgar A. (1977), Product Management: Strategy and

Organization, New York: John Wiley & Sons.

Robertson, Thomas S. (1971), _Innovative Behavior and Communication_, New York: Holt, Rinehart and Winston, Inc.

Robinson, Richard K. (1983), "New Service Development: The Cable TV Connection," in _Emerging Perspectives on Services Marketing_, Leonard L. Berry, G. Lynn Shostack and Gregory Upah, eds., Chicago: American Marketing Association.

Rogers, Everett (1962), _Diffusion of Innovations_, New York: The Free Press.

Rothberg, Robert R., ed. (1981), _Corporate Strategy and Product Innovation_, New York: The Free Press.

Rothwell, Roy (1972), "Factors for Success in Industrial Innovations," from _Project SAPPHO--A Comparative Study of Success and Failure in Industrial Innovation_, Brighton, Sussex: Social Policy Research Unit.

Rubenstein, Albert H., Alok K. Chakrabarti, W. E. Souder, and H. C. Young (1976), "Factors Influencing Innovation Success at the Project Level," _Research Management_ 16 (May), 15-20.

Schon, Donald A. (1971), _Beyond the Stable State_, New York: W. W. Norton & Company.

_____ (1967), _Technology and Change_, New York: Delacorte Press.

Schumpeter, Joseph (1975), _Capitalism, Socialism, and Democracy_, 3rd edition, New York: Harper.

Shostack, G. Lynn (1981), "How to Design a Service," in _Marketing of Services_, James H. Donnelly and William R. George, eds., Chicago: American Marketing Association.

_____ (1977), "Breaking Free From Product Marketing," _Journal of Marketing_, 41 (April), 73-80.

Souder, William E. (1983), "Organizing for Modern Technology and Innovation: A Review and Synthesis," _Technovation_, 2, 27-44.

Tinnesand, Bjornar (1973), "Toward a General Theory of Industrial Innovation," Unpublished PhD dissertation, The University of Wisconsin.

Tushman, Michael L. (1979), "Managing Communication Networks in R&D Laboratories," _Sloan Management Review_, (Winter), 37-49.

Urban, Glen L. and John R. Hauser (1980), _Design and Marketing of New Products_, Englewood Cliffs, N.J.: Prentice-Hall, Inc.

Utterback, James M. (1974), "Innovation in Industry and the Diffusion of Technology," _Science_ 183, 620-626.

Zaltman, Gerald, Robert Duncan, and Jonny Holbek (1973), _Innovations and Organizations_, New York: John Wiley & Sons.

PARTICIPANT PERSPECTIVES ON DEVELOPING
A CLIMATE FOR INNOVATION OF NEW SERVICES
Facilitators:

Bernard H. Booms, Washington State University, Seattle Center
Duane Davis, University of Central Florida
Dennis Guseman, University of Northern Colorado

There was a consensus within the three discussion groups
that a general set of problems exist which are common to all
service industries when developing a climate for innovation of
new services. These problems appear to be similar for both
consumer and industrial services and for regulated and non-
regulated service industries. There was also agreement that
developing a climate for service innovations involves the other
two Symposium topics on service systems and service employees.
The need to include the other two topics suggests that the extensive and growing body of literature on innovation should
distinguish between goods and services because the innovation
process for new services must encompass the issue of simultaneous production of the service by the firm and consumption by
the consumer. This situation expands the importance of the
role of front line employees. The group discussions focused
on both the need for service innovation and facilitation of the
service innovation process.

Need for service innovation

Service firms must compete in rapidly changing environments with increasing pressures from both well-recognized and
nontraditional competitors. Innovations are going to be the
principal means for competing, especially for those firms confronted with deregulation. These competitive pressures are
impacting the service firm both internally which requires extensive organizational structure changes and externally which
focuses new attention on the importance of marketing. Meeting
competitive pressures through innovation holds the potential
for achieving organizational goals for growth and profitability
via new services. Innovation is also instrumental in image
development which is extremely important for firms marketing
intangibles. Finally, it can provide for a better utilization
of physical resources and personnel. Yet any benefits from
innovation cannot be realized without certain prerequisites.

For a service organization to be involved successfully in
the innovation process, first it must be market driven rather

23

than looking to operations for future direction. This requires the innovative firm to recognize the paramount importance of servicing customers' needs. A second requirement is the need for stability within the organization via an accepted mission statement and congruence between guiding beliefs and daily beliefs (see Howard Schwartz's paper). A third prerequisite is a minimum resource base which includes a commitment of funds, personnel and a sufficient time horizon. Once the needs, benefits and prerequisites for service innovation are recognized, the real challenge then becomes how to facilitate the service innovation process.

Facilitating the service innovation process

The three groups spent much of their time brainstorming on what components would most facilitate the innovation process in a service organization. Their ideas can be grouped into three objectives: to obtain top management commitment to innovate, to develop a corporate culture encouraging innovation, and to create systems which facilitate the innovation process. A top management commitment to innovate was considered the critical component. There was a consensus that top management often did not actively promote innovation within the organization. Such a commitment to innovate not only requires the allocation of resources but also a symbolic communication program which lets the entire organization know that top management supports innovation.

A commitment to innovation leads to the development of a corporate culture which encourages innovation. Although substantial attitude changes from the office of the chief executive down to the line employees are beginning to appear, service organizations must move beyond their conservative, reactive responses to the increasing competitive pressures. Instead, they must adopt proactive positions based on an innovative posutre which can serve as guiding beliefs throughout the organization. Over a period of time the daily beliefs should begin to portray innovation as the most profitable competitive response.

A corporate culture which encourages innovation can best be sustained by the creation of systems which facilitate the innovation process. A number of subsystems must evolve here, including organizational structure, employee participation, feedback, internal communications, and reward systems. First, how to integrate the marketing function and operations to achieve a more competitive service organization within an innovative framework is a substantive question. No models are available currently to provide such a framework. While the

24

participants believe that no specific structure is best for all situations, a number of necessary conditions were agreed upon. A formal procedure which generates and evaluates new service ideas is needed. This procedure should encourage innovative ideas at all levels of the organization. All employees should be made aware of the organization's commitment to innovation. Indeed innovation cannot originate from one department or one individual. It must be encouraged throughout the entire organization. Yet formal assignment of the responsibility for the innovation process from the stages of idea generation to commercialization is needed. For example, a new services development department could provide focus and direction throughout the innovation process.

A distinguishing characteristic of the service innovation process (as compared to innovation for goods) is that the design of the service assembly and the implementation of services marketing strategies must always incorporate the public contact employees. Therefore, employee involvement in the innovation process is critical for a service. The Symposium paper by Schneider and Bowen proposes a crucial role for these employees in new services development. This requires more care and attention on how management involves and motivates front line employees to produce and implement new services concepts. Such a broadened involvement of employees in the services innovation process entails significant behavior changes for both the organization and the employee. Management must educate operations employees in terms of marketing concerns and show them why these concerns are important. The focus should be on how an understanding of marketing will help them in their jobs and what this will mean for the organization as a whole. Management must actively solicit employee input during the entire innovation process as well as provide them with ongoing feedback.

Management of a feedback subsystem for both external and internal information is a third consideration for facilitating the innovation process. Externally the organization must monitor the significant shifts occurring in its environment -- e.g. the government, competitors, and customers. Evaluation of customer needs is first qualitative and then quantitative. We must recognize that customers may not know their wants for an intangible until an actual service is available. Yet they should be considered as a primary source of possible innovations. Internal feedback is of two different types: 1. customer satisfaction levels as perceived by the employees who deliver the services; and, 2. employee satisfaction levels as "internal customers" of the firm. Since employees are the critical link between the firm and the customer, they are most

25

likely to hear customer complaints and compliments. Management must encourage and provide methods for them to bring this information back into the organization.

Monitoring employee needs and satisfaction levels is also important. Customers view front line employees as the personae of the total organization. Thus employee satisfaction levels regarding the organization have great impact on how satisfied the ultimate customer will be with the firm's services.

Two final subsystems here are internal communications and the reward system. Achieving effective communications between the various units of the organization is often a difficult problem. But competitive pressures are forcing firms to open up new information flows between and amongst research units, operations, marketing and employees (as service producers and as providers of customer feedback). A reward system for those involved in innovation activities will reinforce the importance of innovative thinking and help generate its future success. Monetary rewards as well as recognition from peers and top management must be viewed by employees as valued incentives in order to induce the behavioral changes necessary.

All of the subsystems for facilitating the innovation process must emerge from a corporate culture and a top management commitment to innovation which will enable the organization to achieve an innovative climate for the development of new services. All subsystems of the corporation-organization structure, employee participation, feedback processes, internal communication and reward systems -- must be managed to reinforce the commitment to innovation.

SERVICE DESIGN IN THE OPERATING ENVIRONMENT

G. Lynn Shostack,
Bankers Trust Company

ABSTRACT

Analysis of case examples suggests that at least ten stages are involved in designing and developing a service. These stages illustrate the complexity of the design process, but also show that a rational, controlled methodology can be established and suggest that a design system with quantified, specific components is feasible.

INTRODUCTION

To work properly, a service development system must have four characteristics. First, it must be objective; not subjective. Second, it must be precise; not vague. Third, it must be fact-driven; not opinion driven. Fourth, it must be methodological; not philosophical. Today, while there are a number of service development theories, there are no service development systems that meet all four criteria.

Interestingly, most of the current literature on services also fails to meet these four criteria. Few writers seem willing to tackle the real essence of a service; i.e., the process itself. Instead, "the service" is dealt with as some sort of metaphysical "concept", or "bundle", and the author moves on to easier topics like employee motivation or internal marketing. The exact nature of the "concept" or "bundle" is left to the imagination, or is further described with vague words and phrases that have no common denominator nor any verifiable validity. The absence of intellectual and analytical rigor in such approaches would be a shock to anyone trained in the scientific method. While poetic labels may be useful in educating the public to the subtle, non-corporeal nature of services, they are not a useful base for service design.

When we deal with services such as investment management, engineering or medicine, we are dealing with process at its most complex. Even services that are easier to grasp, such as barbering or plumbing demand appreciation of the intricacies and variability of process planning and execution. It is here that the essence of service definition, design and development lies.

Both the great behaviorist B. F. Skinner and the great process engineer W. Edwards Deming observed that the key to controlling output was the control of process. Skinner revolutionized psychology by breaking through the prevailing myth that human behavior was pre-programmed via heredity to show that conditioning can have an even more powerful effect. Deming revolutionized manufacturing by rejecting the common belief that workers were to blame for quality problems and demonstrating that the design of the process, not exhortations to "try harder", was the key to productivity.

In both cases, the concepts developed by these pioneers were the result of empiric research, i.e., the direct observation of actual events and the analysis of verifiable facts. Accordingly, to understand service design, we must look to the empiric reality of actual practice. From this, we must attempt to synthesize and draw general conclusions that can be tested in other situations.

For the past year, programmed analysis of a variety of service design and development projects has been underway by the author. During this time, over twelve cases have been followed in detail. Some of these have involved de novo service creation, while others have dealt with service extension, modification and enhancement. Some cases have entailed heavy quantitative documentation, while in others the modus operandi has been entirely verbal. Some projects have been successful; others have done poorly.

What has emerged over time from the combined evidence of these cases is a rational pattern of approach to the service design process. In this paper, one project from the list of those analyzed will be presented to illustrate the flow of events

28

and tasks that occurred during an actual designproject and the stages that emerged as constituting a methodology.

The case concerns the introduction of a discount brokerage service. The design and development of the service took place over a six month period, and the service was introduced to the market in June of 1983. The service was seen as a defensive necessity, to be marketed only to current customers, versus the mass consumer approach adopted by several bank competitors. The design assignment was given to a line officer in an operating division devoted to investment services. The officer was instructed to establish a functioning discount brokerage service within six months. This was the sole initial input.

Over the subsequent six months, a complex cycle was observed, with numerous iterative steps, leading to the service's final form and functionality. Although transitions from one design phase to the next exhibited considerable overlap, ten distinct clusters of activity were discernable. The resultant generalized approach to the design process can be described in the following series of stages.

FIRST LEVEL STAGES

I. First Phase Definition

In the beginning of a service design project, the service definition is usually vague and only a skeletal indication of what the final service will be. Often no written definition exists at this first stage, only a verbal, capsulized "concept". Even when a written description does exist, it is usually a very brief, abstracted statement. The definition is usually functional, i.e., it describes the main results or processes of the service, rather than the implementation structure. Another characteristic of early definition stages is the assumption that all parties involved share a common understanding of the service. As the service assumes a more precise shape, it becomes clear that individual views of the service are not the same. In later phases, negotiation and decision-making are the mechanisms that resolve these design disputes.

In the case of discount brokerage, the service was described as a way "to buy and sell stocks for customers at low prices". As there were numerous discount brokerage services already in existence, it was initially assumed by the project manager that the service to be built was understood by all.

II. First Phase Analysis

In this phase, the information-gathering process begins. A search is made for data and examples relating to the proposed service. Competitors are analyzed, various forms of implementation are identified and dialogue with knowledgeable internal and external parties is initiated. As alternative approaches and features for the service are identified and as new ideas surface, the inadequacy of the First Phase definition becomes apparent.

In the case of discount brokerage, initial investigation revealed numerous alternatives and choices to be made. A wide variety of securities were potential candidates for inclusion in the brokerage service. Each type of security would require staff expertise, have cost implications, and involve systems development time. Some possibilities required joint effort with other operating areas.

Decisions had to be made as to whether all or part of the service should be in-house, joint-ventured or externally contracted. For example, one alternative presupposed maintaining custody of customer securities with an external broker. This had potential service and profit implications, since it would mean giving up direct control of margin loans, an important revenue source. On the other hand, this alternative included an automatic cash sweep to a money market fund, a desirable feature that would have to be built in-house if another vendor were chosen.

Space does not permit a listing of all the options that were surfaced at this phase. Suffice it to say that literally hundreds of issues, small and large, were raised.

III. First Phase Synthesis

At this stage, basic boundaries for the service are drawn. A considerable amount of dialogue and discussion takes place in order to sort out the many alternatives, and, more importantly, to achieve a common understanding of the basic profile of the service to be built. Most of this phase takes place verbally, typically in a series of meetings. The points of view of various parties are clarified. Management typically makes a number of decisions at this stage that are architectural in nature. Certain options are ruled out. This has the effect of clarifying the service definition and limiting the issues that remain to be dealt with.

For example, at this stage, among the conclusions reached regarding discount brokerage were: not to purchase an existing discount brokerage firm, not to surrender custody, and not to include options, futures or municipal bonds in the initial service offering. Other basic decisions involved not incorporating the service into in-house computer systems and the inclusion of an interest-bearing cash account.

SECOND LEVEL STAGES

IV. Second Phase Definition

The First Phase Synthesis makes possible the creation of a detailed service definition.In fact, not until this stage can a meaningful written description be produced that captures the specific features and characteristics that will make the final form of the service unique.

No two services are the same. Even when the outward or superficial evidence appears similar, every service, in its particulars, is different. Services are processes. As such, they are variable. Two firms offering the same service will, upon investigation, be found to have established different process designs for getting there, and each design will pose different constraints and opportunities for changing, expanding and controlling the service.

For example, the choice of systems to produce customer statements may seem to be a mechanical issue, not a marketing issue. Yet one system may allow linkage to other service systems, while another system does not. System linkage can allow new service combinations to be created, which can differentiate an organization's offerings to the market. One system may allow free-form statement messages, while another does not. One may use a laser printer, while another does not. One may be formatted to fit window envelopes, while another requires that envelope labels be produced. Every one of these choices affects the final service's design, and every one of them is a marketing issue.

In the case of discount brokerage, a written design document was produced at this stage that included a structural description of how the service would work, a pro forma financial projection based on pricing strategies derived from cost analysis of the functional design, an implementation plan that included staff requirements, training, control and auditing standards, a market positioning and introduction strategy including advertising/promotion, and a list of remaining issues. At this stage, issues became more and more specific; reaching to detailed levels such as design of customer statements. Even at this stage, hundreds of decisions remained to be made before the service reached its final form.

V. Second Phase Analysis

After a detailed service description is

produced, the service proposal is widely circulated, and its specifics are critiqued in detail. Attention is focused on operational factors, the identification of flaws in the design and the raising of any remaining issues or problems. Potential fail points are identified and failsafe or corrective processes are designed to counter them. Execution and productivity standards are set. These are often a function of work measurement techniques.

Second Phase Analysis is usually more productive than First Phase Analysis, because it is based on a concrete and specific service blueprint. The more detailed the model, the easier it is to respond with constructive and specific feedback. Compared to abstract and generalized First Phase definitions, the second phase brings a service virtually to the point of implementation.

Thorough Second Phase Analysis is especially important, and exposing the proposal to the rigor of line criticism is vital. If the design is critiqued in a vacuum or a "planning" laboratory, not only are the conclusions likely to be biased toward the planner's preconceived wishes, but the service will almost certainly encounter implementation problems due to oversights and superficial analysis.

Focused market research may also be done at this stage, giving prospective customers an opportunity to respond to the proposal and provide input to the design process. Market research done at earlier stages is usually worthless, since it only provides reaction to a vague abstraction. The market can provide actionable feedback only when it is given actionable input.

In the case of discount brokerage, Second Phase Analysis revealed a number of unexpected design issues. For example, the blueprint proposed a pricing schedule based on both number of shares or bonds traded and the value of the security. This was consistent with competitors' pricing. However, a question was raised by one reviewer as to the rationale for this pricing method. On further analysis, it was determined that market value had virtually nothing to do with the costs of execution. As a result, the pricing was simplified to be soley a function of numbers of securities traded. This schedule was not only easier for customers to understand than competitors' prices, it yielded the added benefit of making the internal commission calculation process simpler and therefore less costly. Other results of Second Phase Analysis included the development of a customer card with a telephone trading number and customer account number, a methodology for setting interest rates on customer cash balances, and the specification of interface mechanisms with the outside vendors that had been chosen to handle execution and account records.

VI. Second Phase Synthesis

This stage represents the final pre-implementation blueprint. The revised service description is documented, often in a lengthy volume covering all aspects of the service. In this phase, commitments are made and contracts signed. Staff hiring begins, and the first work begins to prepare marketing materials.

Second Phase Synthesis will trigger the preparation of detailed implementation sub-plans. A team is synthesized consisting of all the accountable parties. Each area that will be involved in rendering the service will work from the final blueprint, translating it to the lowest level in the organization.

The blueprint will now be frozen until the post-implementation audit.

THE FINAL STAGES

VII. First Phase Implementation

In this stage, the operational functions of the service are put in place. First Phase Implementation requires a separate plan drawn from the final service blueprint. This sub-plan includes time and deliverable schedules based on working backward from the desired introduction date. As is true in all other phases of service design, hundreds of specific issues must be addressed, and every detail must be taken seriously. Staff must be housed and trained, procedures written, performance standards defined and the entire process debugged. It is in this phase that delays such as in telephone installations and delivery of the wrong equipment occur.

If possible, first phase implementation should include an operating test of the service. This is similar to product testing or market testing in a product environment. Formal testing of services is not a widespread phenomenon. Few companies are willing to invest the considerable sums required to prototype a functioning service, because they perceive little difference between the costs in labor, systems and set-up of going "live", and the costs of limited trial. Such logic is, of course, completely fallacious.

Instead of a pilot test, actual market introduction is often the first real test of functionality and market acceptance. By that point, mistakes in design are harder to correct and service modifications needed in order to improve acceptance or operating efficiency are more laborious to implement. There is simply no substitute for a proper rehearsal.

In the case of discount brokerage, a pilot was run by offering employees a special price for one month on new accounts. The offer was marketed internally and the test period allowed observation of the process in action prior to its market debut. Even at this stage, minor changes and fine tuning of the process was done as operating experience showed several areas in which the service was not as smooth as it could be.

VIII. Second Phase Implementation

After the entire service process is established, the service is ready for market introduction. In this stage, advertising, direct mail, publicity and service evidence such as customer statements and advices are prepared. As is true throughout the service design and development cycle, each phase represents many complex processes. The development of advertising/promotion programs, for example, is a full time activity that, for some services, may consume as much time as the design itself.

For discount brokerage, the advertising/promotion program was modest in scale, and based primarily on mailer inserts to checking account statements. Preparation for market introduction also included many final rehearsals and a great deal of internal work. For example, legal staff finalized contract wording, auditors completed their program standards, accounting and M.I.S. mechanisms were put in place, and the personnel unit finished its training, job description and goal-setting tasks.

IX. Market Introduction

The service goes live. Telephones ring, inquiries are answered, accounts are opened. Transactions are executed. Statements are mailed.

During the first stages of market introduction, it is vitally important that all parts of the service be closely monitored. Closely monitored means that every phone call is recorded and followed up to determine why accounts are or are not being opened. It means that every transaction is logged, every employee's throughput is tracked, every glitch is isolated.

This research should go on long enough to cover at least several complete cycles of the service. If it takes the customer six months to experience all aspects of the service, then monitoring should cover six months before the next phase is reached.

Many services are virtually thrown willy nilly into the market place. Whether they function as they were designed to function, or function well or poorly seems to be of little concern. Considering the extraordinary labor that goes into creating a service, it is a pity when a service is abandoned at the point of its birth.

There are product analogues for this sort of sloppiness, but they are rare among the great package goods companies, who have learned the value of and practice highly refined post-introduction research.

Nevertheless, some products have been launched with no follow-up monitoring, and their stories are generally sad ones. The Apple III computer, for example, which is an exceptionally fine machine, was shipped and then found to be functionally flawed. Although this should have been caught at the manufacturing or testing stage, it certainly should have been caught well before the machine was widely distributed, and would have been had there been good product introduction follow up. Instead, the product was tarred with bad publicity. A subsequent recall and correction of the problems was not enough to change the market's view that the machine was flawed. Today, the Apple III is a market failure.

In the case of discount brokerage, extensive monitoring of all phases of live operation was done. Careful tracking of customer contact points, market response and operating efficiency led to the assembly of detailed documentation on the soundness of the underlying design, and the relationship of real events to the model.

X. Post-Introduction Audit

In this stage, the data gathered during the Implementation Stage is synthesized and corrections are made to the service. Also at this stage, the next steps for modifying or enhancing the service are identified, and the design/development cycle begins again.

No service is fixed or immutable. A constant process of change and evolution, whether deliberate or inadvertent, is always occurring. When the design process is thorough, this evolution is controlled. When design is ad hoc, evolution is random.

In the case of discount brokerage, one interesting and unanticipated fail point showed up after the first operating month, and it is a good example of how incomplete service design can affect market perceptions of a service. A monthly market rate of interest was paid on cash balances. This rate was set according to internal formulas and communicated by phone to the external vendor, who handled transaction and statement processing, to be fed into a program that calculated and posted the interest. This communication process failed. The wrong interest rate was input, customer statements were mailed, and then had to be remailed with the correct rate and an apology. Needless to say, it was embarrassing. The potential for failure should have been identified during the design cycle and wasn't. Secondarily, it should have been caught by spot checking statements prior to mailing.

However, as is so often the case, assumptions were made that this simple procedure would function properly. Immediately upon the discovery that it didn't, a new process was implemented that included written confirmation of the rate to be paid as well as spot checks of statements prior to mailing.

For discount brokerge, the next steps of service evolution also were identified at this stage. Proposals were made to include options, futures and municipal bonds, as well as to shift money market trading accounts to the discount brokerage account. The design/development process is never ending and iterative. We have arrived at Phase I again.

THE FINAL SERVICE

A simplified blueprint of the service that was introduced is shown in Figure 1. As can be seen, very little of the actual service is visible to the customer. In fact, as is the case with many services, customers have virtually no idea of the processes that underlie most services. And yet, these processes <u>are</u> the service. The tangible evidence seen by the consumer is only the visible tip. Such tangible evidence has no value whatsoever independent of the service.

Discount brokerage is not an especially complex service. Even so, the blueprint shown in Figure 1 has been considerably condensed and simplified relative to its complete form. Every step shown on the blueprint is actually a series of sub-processes. A step such as "Prepare and Mail", for example, requires many activities and participants, and includes over ten separate stages from production and control of laser printing to stuffing and sealing envelopes. No marketer should assume that these or any other components of a service are trivial or unworthy of attention and concern. I have seen a whole image campaign undone by statement envelopes containing confidential customer data that popped open in transit due to inferior glue.

The initial discount brokerage blueprint covers only listed stocks and bonds. Each kind of investment that is added will complicate the service, for such assets as options, futures and municipal bonds each have unique requirements. However, each can now be diagrammed onto the basic design, and the entire process will proceed more rapidly for future enhancements. Additionally, internal audit, accounting and MIS links are not shown. These are equally vital to management of the service.

As shown, only the major fail points of the service have been highlighted. These are the areas most likely to cause execution or consistency problems. Telephone communication, for example, is difficult to control. Yet this is one of the most powerful shapers of the customer's perception. Accordingly, special care was taken to script dialogue for all possible situations, to ensure that telephones never went unanswered, and to assure accuracy of content through recording of all instructions from customers.

Execution standards are also shown. These represent the main throughput targets for the service. For example, an advice should go out within 24 hours of a purchase or sale. Such standards can be monitored and audited.

GENERAL CONCLUSIONS

From the foregoing description of the design and development of a real service, a number of observations can be made.

First, the process of designing and developing a service is exceedingly complex. The description of actual events given in this paper is a severely condensed one. If fully documented, this author estimates that over one hundred pages of text would be needed to trace the entire process.

Second, the process is iterative and largely definitional. The objective of service design is to establish a totally specific and rational definition of the process. Through iteration, decisions are made that make the profile more and more specific, until all the means for creating the service have been defined.

Third, a great deal of the process is verbal and word bound. As the project progresses, an expanding circle of people becomes involved. This process and the dialogue that accompanies it have the effect of building successive and more refined mental portraits.

One management factor that seems to be important is limiting and controlling the expanding circle, so that each stage is properly completed before new parties are brought in to the design process. One element of projects that did not do well seems to be that too many people were involved in early phases. Conversely, projects which were developed entirely by staff or "planners" did not do well either. The key appears to be to begin with a limited number of people and to add others only when their roles can be clearly defined. At each stage, the importance of translating verbal input into pictorial or quantitative terms is critical. This provides the objective benchmark for subsequent input and prevents the service from becoming murky and consensus-driven.

Fourth, every service is unique. The design process itself shows that it is so complex, the probabilities of any two services arriving at precisely the same design are virtually nil. Many things from environment to people add variations. It is in these subtle differences that differentiation often lies.

Finally, whether the process is fully documented or not, good service design seems to require that all ten stages be completed. Projects that fail seem to be those that skip stages or gloss over them. And service problems appear to be traceable directly to stages that were not properly or thoroughly executed.

In sum, case experience would suggest that the design and development of a service can be made rational, objective, methodological and precise. While the foregoing does not offer a complete system, it strongly indicates that one can be developed which will apply to services other than those constituting the body of this investigation. Such a system would be of great utility to all service marketers and additional work on the subject should be a high priority in both the academic and business worlds.

DISCOUNT BROKERAGE

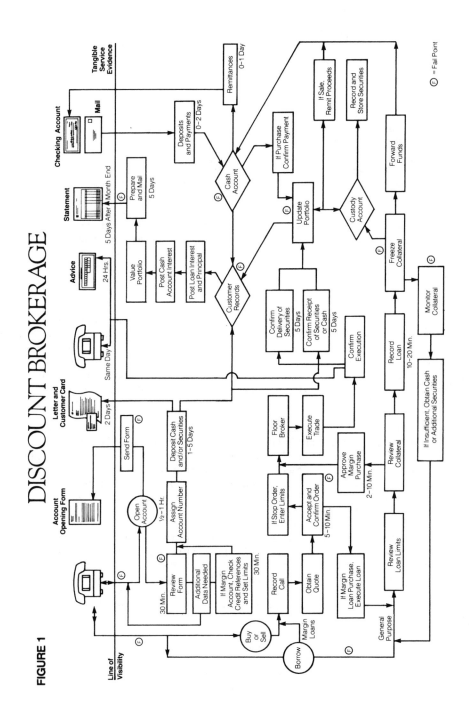

FIGURE 1

43

DEVELOPING AND IMPLEMENTING NEW SERVICES

Christopher H. Lovelock, Harvard University

ABSTRACT

Service marketers can learn much about the new product development process from existing studies of innovation management in the manufacturing sector. However, distinctive issues for managers in service organizations include understanding the factors that motivate or facilitate new service development, searching for new service ideas, evaluating new product "fit", blueprinting the design of the new service and its delivery system, and managing the implementation process as it relates to integrating different management functions and obtaining the desired behavior from customers.

INTRODUCTION

The topic of developing and introducing new products has long been regarded as very important among both marketing academics and professionals. The literature on this topic is enormous, reflecting extensive research and widespread sharing of insights from experience. Virtually every marketing principles text devotes an obligatory chapter - or at least a major section of a chapter - to new products.

This fact poses some problems for a symposium on developing new services, where the natural desire of many participants is to focus on issues that are distinctive to services rather than to rehash generalizations from past research that focused almost exclusively on new manufactured goods. However, I think it would be a mistake to ignore the useful conceptual frameworks that we already have.

Instead, I'd like to begin by reviewing some key concepts and frameworks from the general literature and then considering what other writers have had to say about new services development. From that starting point, I'll proceed to raise additional issues tailored to the concerns of service organizations and offer some insights for managers of specific types of services.

DEGREES OF PRODUCT INNOVATION

The word "new" is perhaps one of the most overused in the marketer's lexicon. Heany (1983) rightfully calls attention to the danger of semantic inflation with regard to product innovation. He proposes six categories of product innovation within a spectrum that runs from major innovations to style changes. These categories are described below with service sector examples added.

1. Major Innovations are new products for markets as yet undefined and undimensioned. Past examples include the first broadcast television services and Federal Express's introduction of nationwide, overnight small package delivery service. These innovations involve a high degree of uncertainty, not least in terms of market response.

2. Start-up Businesses consist of new products for a market that is already served by existing products that meet the same generic needs. Service examples include: the creation of health maintenance organizations to provide an alternative form of health care delivery; Merrill Lynch's creation of the Cash Management Account that combines brokerage, debit card, and bank checking services in a single package; and the entry of telecommunication companies into the long-distance household telephone call market previously restricted to the Bell System.

3. New Products for the Currently Served Market represent an attempt to offer existing customers of the organization a product not previously available there (although it may be available elsewhere). Examples include: retail banks that add insurance services or money-market funds, or museums that add restaurants or shops to their exhibit facilities.

4. Product Line Extensions represent an augmentation of the existing product line, such as adding new menu items for a restaurant, new routes for an airline, or new courses of study at a university. Offering a new self-service option, such as an automatic teller machine (ATM) at a bank or a self-serve island at a gas station effectively constitute product-line extensions.

5. Product Improvements represent perhaps the commonest type of product innovation, involving a change in certain features for products that are already on offer to the currently served market. In the service sector these may include not only improvements to the core service, such as faster execution of service, but also peripheral changes such as automatically providing bank customers with their account balances after each deposit and withdrawal at an ATM, or improvements in service delivery achieved by extending hours of availability or increasing the number of outlets.

6. Style Changes represent the most modest type of product innovation, although they are often highly visible. Thus an air-

45

line may paint its aircraft in a new color scheme, a hotel may put its employees into new uniforms, or a bank may refurbish its branch interiors or introduce a new design of checks.

When speaking of new product development, we need to be clear what level of innovation is being discussed. As a generalization, the higher the level of innovation, the greater the risks and expenses entailed and the more difficult the managerial task. All innovations require effort in evaluation planning, and execution. The resources allocated to these efforts should reflect the degree of uncertainty involved, the downside risks, the upside potential for the organization, the extent of management coordination involved, and the time horizon required for effective implementation.

PRODUCT EVALUATION AND LIFE CYCLE

In nearly all successful marketing organizations, the composition of the product portfolio is slowly but continuously evolving. Likewise, the characteristics of the individual products making up that portfolio are themselves undergoing change. Both processes reflect the need to be responsive to the dynamics of the marketplace, since external factors in the environment - the economy, technology, government policies, social structures and values, and competitive forces - are constantly changing.

As each planning cycle begins - and sometimes more frequently if sudden external changes occur - the marketing manager needs to consider the following issues.
1. Are we offering the appropriate mix of products in our portfolio or is a shift in emphasis needed? Should new products be added or existing ones deleted?
2. Are we currently offering (or planning to introduce) products with the right characteristics to appeal to our target market segments, or are changes needed in product attributes?
3. Do the other elements in the current marketing-mix strategy for each product - distribution and delivery systems, monetary prices and nonmonetary costs, and communication efforts - reflect a cost-efficient (and, where appropriate, competitive) approach to marketing the product to our target market segments? If not, what changes should we be making in our marketing mix?

It is important to remember that no decision can be taken on product strategy without reference to how that product should be priced, delivered, and communicated to its effective market segments. Effective marketing strategy requires consistency and synergy between each element of the marketing mix; hence decisions concerning any one element must be evaluated against

46

their impact on - and must fit with - the other three. As will be shown, there is often an extremely close link in service organizations between the product and its delivery system.

Product Evolution

Marketing theorists are constantly looking for conceptual frameworks that will help practicing managers better understand the nature of the problems and opportunities they face.

One intriguing approach is to consider the evolution of species, as described by the theory of natural selection, as a model for the evolution of products in a competitive marketplace (Gross 1968). Appraising this analogy, Wind remarks:

The basic concepts of the Darwinian natural selection theory and marketing concepts are strikingly similar. The individual organism in the evolution theory is analogous to a product (not product class...). The concept of a <u>variation of species</u> is analogous to the differences among products and brands. The concept of overpopulation relates to the tremendous production capacity for most products. The <u>struggle for existence</u> and <u>survival of the fittest</u> are quite descriptive of the product marketplace in which only few new products ever make it. The result of overcapacity (overpopulation) is competition among species (products). In this competition, those best suited to the <u>environment</u> (the marketplace) have the best chance for success (survival and growth). (Wind 1982, p. 64).

A number of useful managerial insights are suggested by this analogy. For instance, specialization (typically entailing a carefully designed product-positioning strategy) undoubtedly offers an advantage under conditions of strong competition. However, as the environment changes, the characteristics that determine suitability also change, requiring evolutionary development of the product so that it may adapt; this emphasizes the need for long-range product planning. When the environment changes suddenly - reflecting such factors as significant technological, economic, or political developments - highly specialized products that were well adapted to the old environment may be less capable of adjusting to the change than less specialized products. "This conclusion," says Wind, "suggests the intriguing hypothesis that products aimed at narrow market segments or very specialized applications have shorter 'life cycles' than more broadly-based products."

Recent rethinking of Darwinian theory suggests that evolution may have been less gradual than Darwin believed, consisting more of a series of sudden, discontinuous spurts in response to dramatic environmental changes. This is also, perhaps, a better

47

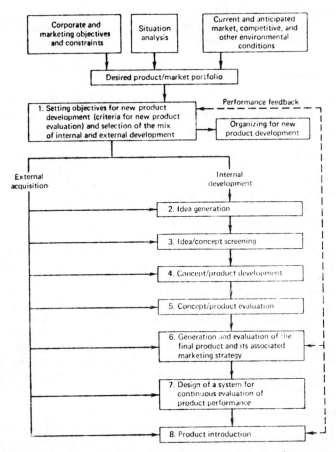

Figure 1   New-product-development system. (From Wind 1982).

model of the marketplace for the products of service organizations, faced as they are with sudden shifts of the regulatory environment, changes in professional association standards, the ups and downs of the economy, and the periodic advent of new technology. The key difference between animal species and product species lies in the fact that animals can only react to change. Managers, however, can anticipate change and take proactive steps to enhance their products' prospects for future survival. The sum of all the products offered by an organization is the organization itself; that, too, must evolve and change over the years if it is to survive as an entity.

The Product Life Cycle

Complementing the product-evolution model is another conceptual framework, the product life cycle (PLC), which is based on the biological life cycle of birth, growth, maturity, decline, and death. It can be applied to an individual product or to an entire class of related products produced by a number of different competing organizations.

Most marketing theorists divide the PLC into four stages.

1. Introduction. A period of typically slow growth in sales volume following the launch ("birth") of the product. At this point, an innovative organization that is the first to market the product may have the field to itself. However, extensive communication efforts are often needed to build consumer awareness.

2. Growth. Demand for the product begins to increase rapidly, reflecting repeated use by satisfied customers and broadening awareness among prospective customers who now try the product for the first time. Competition develops as other organizations introduce their own versions, transforming a single product into a product class of competing brands. Since few service organizations are able to obtain patent protection for their innovations, competition often develops very rapidly in the service sector.

3. Maturity. This is often an extended period (except for fad and fashion products) during which sales volume for the product class stabilizes and astute marketers seek to position their own product offerings in ways that will differentiate them from those of competing organizations.

4. Decline. Sales volume for the product class declines as a result of environmental forces such as changing population profiles, changing consumer preferences, new legislation, or competion from new types of products that meet the same generic need. Some competitors, anticipating the death of the entire product class, kill off their own entries in the market.

The appeal of the PLC concept to marketers is that it provides a marketing-strategy prescription tailored to the stage in the life cycle that the product has currently reached. However, a quick review of the PLC literature reveals that its presciptive insights are directed primarily at consumer packaged goods.

PRODUCT-LINE ADDITIONS, DELETIONS, AND MODIFICATIONS

Few service organizations face a static, unchanging market for their products. Most marketplaces are dynamic - changes in customer needs and behavior and in the number and mix of customers occur; competitors enter and exit; technological changes influence product features and delivery systems. Products that advanced the institutional mission well 10 years ago may be outmoded, uncompetitive, or even irrelevant today. Some will need to be discarded and others improved or reconstituted. To fulfill the mission well 10 years (or less) from now may require development of new product offerings that will be attuned to the needs and opportunities of the times.

NEW PRODUCT DEVELOPMENT

Many new products prove to be a disappointment to their sponsors, failing to advance the institutional mission, diverting management time and attention, generating a new cash drain on the organization's finances - or perhaps all of these. Managers who have had bad luck with new products in the past often become averse to risk as a result. But no organization can afford to stagnate, and not introducing any new products at all may prove as damaging to the institution's health as selecting the wrong new products or botching the introduction process.

The issue of designing and marketing new products has attracted great interest from both managers and academics. Excellent syntheses and new insight are provided by Urban and Hauser (1980) and Wind (1982). There is generally agreement that the new-product-development process should proceed systematically through a series of steps, beginning with a review of corporate (institutional) objectives and constraints and continuing through to product introduction. Figure 1 (drawn from Wind 1982) summarizes these steps in diagrammatic form. As can be seen, there are three major sets of inputs:

1. Corporate and marketing objectives.
2. The organization's strengths and weaknesses - assessed by conducting a marketing audit (see Kotler, Gregor, and Rodgers 1977).
3. Information on the current and anticipated market, the competitive situation and other environmental factors (also assessed via the marketing audit).

From these inputs, management can derive an indication of what the desired product portfolio for the organization should look like. By comparing this "ideal" with the current portfolio, gaps and opportunities can be quickly identified. Objectives can then be set for new-product development and suitable criteria established for evaluating prospective candidates. Later we will look at some specific factors spurring innovation in the service sector.

New products can be developed entirely in-house or through external acquisition. Thus a merger might take place between two service businesses with complementary products, or a service

50

firm that was strong in one geographic area might seek to acquire similar firms in other geographic areas. In either case, a carefully managed process is needed, first, to ensure that good ideas are not overlooked and, second, to subject the ideas that are generated to a rigorous screening process.

Ideas that pass the initial screening (stage 3 or the sequence in Figure 1) then move to a more formal conceptualization and are developed into a specific product proposal (Step 4). At this point, the proposed product is still likely to be in conceptual form but should be sufficiently clearly defined that consumer reactions can be sought to specific features and a management evaluation made of the proposed product's technical feasibility, economic implications, market potential, and congruence with management objectives (Step 5). Truly innovative new products are particularly at risk during this stage since they involve higher risks, are less likely to be compatible with current procedures and objectives, and may not be readily understood by prospective customers.

Step 6 is a difficult one. As Wind (1982) writes, "The transformation of new product concepts (which survived the screening and evaluation stages) into actual products is one of the most challenging tasks in the new product development process. This transformation typically involves the conversion of verbally stated (and occasionally pictorially presented) product features into a product prototype, package, brand name, and associated services such as warranty or after sales services" (p. 338). As we will show, it is often difficult to develop prototypes of services since such products are basically processes or performances, rather than things or objects. This stage involves not only definition of the final product but also specification of how that product will be priced, distributed, and communicated to target customers.

The last two stages in Wind's version of the new product development process involve design of a system for continuous evaluation of product performance and, finally, product introduction.

Evaluating Product Fit

Throughout the new-product-development process the product must be evaluated in terms of how well it fits the marketing environment. This evaluation should continue at regular intervals throughout the product's life. There are two basic dimensions to product fit:

1. Product-organization fit.
2. Product-market fit.

Product-organization fit raises such questions as how well
the product matches the institutional mission and what its impact will be on the organization's financial situation. There
are also questions relating to the fit with other existing resource inputs, including labor, management skills, and physical
facilities. Lastly, the product must be evaluated against each
element in the organization's current marketing mix, requiring
consideration of such questions as:

- Is the proposed new service a logical extension of the existing product line? Will it complement existing products
  or "cannibalize" them by eating into their sales?
- Are the monetary price and payment terms compatible with
  those for existing products? What are the implications
  for a public or nonprofit organization of introducing
  (say) a fee-based service when previously all its services
  have been offered free of charge?
- Can existing channels of distribution or delivery systems
  be used, or will it be necessary to add new outlets and
  new intermediaries?
- What communications strategies will be needed to inform
  prospective customers about the product? Is it possible
  to "piggyback" information about the product on existing
  sales calls or advertising messages, or must new communications programs be developed - perhaps requiring use of
  unfamiliar media and communication techniques?

Product-market fit is concerned with how well the new product matches customer needs, interests, and purchase/adoption
procedures. Unless the product represents a significant innovation, the question must be asked: does it have sufficient advan-
tages over already established competing products that customers
will be prepared to switch? Can the organization reach prospective customers with the information they need about the product?
Can customers afford the cost in terms of money and time? Will
they be turned off by the facilities, by other customer using
the service, or by some other perceived psychic costs associated
with the product? Are customers likely to patronize the locations in which the product will be distributed at the specific
times that it is scheduled to be available? Even if the product
appears to fit well with prospective customers, do competing
products fit even better? Will introduction of the product result in a competitive retaliation to which the organization cannot adequately respond?

ORGANIZING AND MANAGING THE DEVELOPMENT EFFORT

Urban and Hauser (1980) and Wind (1982) devote considerable
space in their books to how best to organize and manage new pro-

duct development efforts. Both recognize the importance of top
management involvement and the need for interfunctional coordination and continuity over time. Both present alternative formal
organization models but recognize the significance of informal
roles and relationships in successful execution. Urban and
Hauser identify eight informal roles that need to be filled and
played well:

1. Champion - an advocate who champions the new product and
sells it internally, overcoming objections and generating the
energy and resources necessary to see it through.

2. Protector - a senior manager who defends the champion's right
to advocate the new product, facilitates the latter's efforts to
sell the concept internally, and provides legitimacy and maturity for the product development effort.

3. Auditor - an individual who balances the champion's enthusiasm by ensuring that the product will meet corporate objectives
and that sales forecasts are realistic and accurate.

4. Controller - an individual responsible for watching schedules
and budgets. The controller should be willing to treat past
inputs to a project as sunk costs, allocating new funds solely
on the basis of anticipated future results.

5. Creator/Inventor - creative managers and scientists who will
design and market new products if nourished and supported in an
environment that doesn't impose too many constraints.

6. Leader - the manager (not necessarily the champion) who re-
cruits, teaches, and motivates the new product development team,
as well as interfacing with other parts of the organization by
acting as a translator and integrator.

7. Strategist - the new product development effort requires a
senior manager or planner who possesses a long-run managerial
perspective. This individual recognizes that innovation is
needed not for its own sake but for its ability to help the organization achieve its long-term goals.

8. Judge - an individual who resolves differences of opinion
concerning new product introduction in situations where concen-
sus cannot be arrived at through mediation.

These roles seem as appropriate for innovations from the
service sector as from manufacturing. In my view, the roles
of champion, protector, and leader may be particular important
for new services when the initiative for the innovation comes
from marketing and is resisted by operations personnel.

PAST RESEARCH INTO NEW SERVICES DEVELOPMENT

The literature on new service development is limited, especially when it comes to developing generalizations across service industries. The principal studies of interest are by Wind (1982), Shostack (1981), and Langeard et al. (1981)

Wind (1982)

Although most of Wind's book is based on studying new consumer goods, he indicates that most goods require some supporting services and that services often have marketing characteristics similar to goods. Hence, the principles of new product development should be equally applicable to services. However, Wind cites a few distinctive characteristics of services that are likely to have an impact on new service research and development systems (pp.550-551).

Specifically, he cites the intangibility of services as making in-home tests not very meaningful for services that don't require supporting physical goods and suggests that it may be more appropriate to move directly from concept testing to test marketing or its alternatives. Then he notes that difficulty in patenting services increases the ease of competitive entry, reducing the incentive for large R&D investments and focusing new service development efforts on "me-too" products or improvements to existing services. Problems in achieving standardization, he says, make it difficult to develop accurate concept descriptions and increase the uncertainty involved in projecting market performance from concept test results.

A further distinction concerns the direct relationships between client and service provider found in many services; this argues for conducting research that can obtain information on clients' desired interaction with the service delivery system. Finally, says Wind, the lack of clear demarcation lines between the outlet and product components of many services poses difficulties for concept/product testing, since customers must combine new product decisions with choices of outlet. Will people adopt a new service from a new supplier, possibly purchasing all their service needs from the innovator, as opposed to waiting for the existing supplier to add the new service later?

Shostack (1981)

Shostack's past contribution to our understanding of new service development focus on the product evaluation stage. Although a mock-up or prototype can be made of a physical good or of a facility associated with the delivery of a service, the actual service performance can only exist in blueprint form until the concept is made operational. Essentially, the marketer must understand what processes must take place for the service to be performed satisfactorily for prospective customers in each of the segments targeted. Figure 2, adapted from Shostack, displays a blueprint for a simple service such as a corner shoeshine, standard execution times for each step, the customer's estimated tolerance for delays in execution, and specification of the facilitating goods and services required.

(A) Process of Product Execution

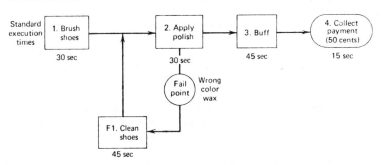

(B) Facilitating Elements

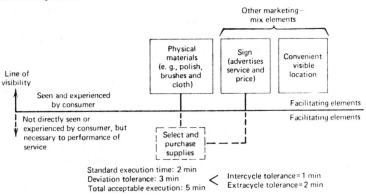

Figure 2: Blueprinting a simple service: a street corner shoeshine (expanded from Shostack 1981)

Describing this model, Shostack writes: "The basic requirements of a service blueprint are three. First, since processes take place in time, the blueprint must, like PERT charting, show time dimensions in diagrammatic form.

"Second, like methods engineering, the blueprint must identify and handle errors, bottlenecks, recycling steps, etc.

55

"Finally, usually after research, the blueprint must precisely define the tolerance of the model, i.e., the degree of variation from the blueprint's standards that can be allowed in execution without affecting the consumer's perception of overall quality and timeliness."

Langeard, Bateson, Lovelock, and Eiglier (1981)

Langeard et al. examine several different services—retail banking, restaurants, travelers checks, airline travel, lodging, and gasoline service stations—with primary emphasis on the first two. Their study emphasizes innovations in service delivery procedures that require customers to perform certain services for themselves, rather than having service personnel do it for them. These innovations include automatic teller machines (ATMs), quick service restaurants, travelers' check dispensing machines, and self-service gasoline pumps. The authors examine not only consumer attitudes towards adoption but also views on implementation by both head office and field managers.

This study draws a distinction between the service operations system, which is divided into those aspects of the production process that are visible to consumers and those that are invisible, and the service delivery system, which comprises visible operations personnel and facilities plus other customers using the service at the same time. As far as the customer is concerned, the service delivery system is the product.

Among the conclusions reached by Langeard et al. are the following:

1. Consumer willingness to consider the self service innovation is strongly dependent upon situational factors (such as time of day, presence of absence of others accompanying the decision-maker, type of clothes worn, and so forth). Concept testing must include definition of relevant situational variables, otherwise prospective consumers are likely to respond simply that "it all depends. . .. "

2. Both time savings and monetary savings are important motivators, either singly or jointly, for using the self service option.

3. Management's perceptions of consumer preferences and intentions are frequently inaccurate, emphasizing the importance of conducting research as opposed to simply relying on managerial judgments.

4. Whereas the emphasis for technologically innovative delivery systems in banking (such as ATMs) often comes from operations,

the impetus for new menu items in chain restaurants tends to come from marketing. The former function tends to focus on opportunities for cost savings and improved efficiency, the latter on adding value for consumers without full understanding of the operational implications.

5. New services involving customer interaction with equipment can be tested under laboratory conditions, using prototypes of the equipment operated by a sample of representative prospective users. Unobtrusive observation and subsequent interviews are useful research devices.

6. Successful development and implementation of a new service requires effective coordination of efforts between marketing and operations.

DISTINCTIVE ISSUES FOR SERVICE MARKETERS

The discussion thus far has emphasized that service marketers can learn much about the new product development process from existing concepts, analytical frameworks, and strategic insights based primarily upon studies of innovation management in the manufacturing sector. However, recent research indicates that services do have some distinctive characteristics that require modification of traditional approaches to new product development.

In the remainder of this paper, I want to offer some further thoughts about the new service development process as these relate to the following aspects of that process:

- o Understanding the factors that motivate or facilitate new service development
- o Searching for new service ideas
- o Evaluating new product "fit"
- o Blueprinting the design of the new service and its delivery system, and
- o Managing the implementation process as it relates to integrating different management functions and obtaining the desired behavior from customers

Factors Motivating or Facilitating New Service Development

Most of the factors initating a need for new goods also apply to services. Urban and Hauser (1980) list corporate objectives such as financial goals, sales growth, competitive standing, and extension of product life cycle, as well as technology, invention, regulation, material costs and availability demographic and lifestyle changes, and customer requests. I'd like to comment on a couple of these and add some additional ones.

Technology creates opportunities for new or enhanced services in several ways: (1) new goods - such as videotape recorders or CAT scanners--are developed and a rental service may grow up to make them more widely available; (2) new equipment, such as automatic teller machines or supersonic aircraft, makes possible new or faster delivery systems for existing services: (3) electronic data banks, coupled with suitable updating, search, and access systems, allow creation of information retrieval services; (4) on-line connections to centralized data banks allow creation of electronic delivery channels to remote locations where financial and other information-based services can be delivered in real-time through branches, intermediaries, or self-service machines; (5) new technologies present a need for expert consulting, repair, and maintenance services.

Deregulation. Partial or complete deregulation in the U.S. of such service industries as banking and other financial services, transportation, and telecommunications has allowed firms to enter new geographic markets, offer products previously prohibited to them, and spurred innovations such as bundling of several related services into a synergistic package (e.g. the Cash Management Account that combines brokerage, checking, and debit card facilities).

Elimination of Professional Association Restrictions Changes in legal, medical, accounting, and architectural codes of "professional ethics" to allow advertising have spurred development of new services and innovative delivery systems such as health maintenance organizations, franchise chains of small business accounting services, and legal clinics in shopping malls.

Growth of Franchising. As one-time "Mom & Pop" service outlets are displaced by or absorbed into large franchise chains, a centralized management function is created. This spurs formal research into service innovations, product line extensions, product enhancement, and opportunities for new delivery systems. The consolidation of information into a centralized data bank may also have the effect of creating an information service of value to customers. Examples include nationwide real estate or employment listing services for geographically mobile clients.

Balancing Supply and Demand. Capacity-constrained services that face significant fluctuations in demand find themselves in a feast or famine situation: either business is turned away because demand exceeds supply, or expensive equipment and staff stand idle because demand is well below the operation's capacity. This situation provokes a need to develop new, countercyclical services that will use productive capacity in periods of previously low demand (e.g. Alpine slides in summer to stimulate

use of chair-lifts that carry skiers in winter). It also encourages development of reservation services (often supplied
by intermediaries) and services that occupy customers' time
while they are queuing (e.g. a bar for restaurant patrons waiting for a table to become available).

Searching for New Service Ideas

Many services fall into one of the following three categories: (1) rental of equipment and/or facilities that the customer doesn't own; (2) hire of labor or expertise that the customer does not possess (or choose to exercise); (3) rental of both
equipment and/or facilities, and the personnel required for
their operation. In each instance, using the service is an alternative to owning the item or doing the work oneself. Thinking constructively about such alternatives may suggest opportunities for new services that perform the task better or more
economically.

Figure 3, taken from Lovelock (1984) illustrates how services often compete with manufactured goods to deliver the same
generic benefits.

Services as Substitutes for Owning
and/or Using Goods (Lovelock, 1984)

	Own a Physical Good	Rent the Use of a Physical Good
Perform the Work Oneself	• Drive Your Own Car • Type on Your Own Typewriter	• Rent a Car and Drive It • Rent a Typewriter and Type on It
Hire Someone to do the Work	• Hire Chauffeur to Drive Your Car • Hire a Typist to Use Your Typewriter	• Hire a Taxi or Limousine • Send Out Work to a Typing Agency

Figure 3

In this diagram, the examples shown are for consumer goods and
services, but comparable industrial/institutional products--
such as truck fleets and computers--could easily be substitut-
ed. The Yellow Pages are full of firms both large and small
that rent equipment and expertise as an alternative to owning
it and doing it in-house.

Another source of new service ideas comes from manufacturing firms with in-house service departments (such as repair and maintenance, education, advertising services, research, credit, consulting, and so forth). A number of firms which developed these services to facilitate the sales of their own manufactured goods have since sought to make them available to customers who did not purchase original equipment from the firm. As a result, new profit centers or subsidiary companies may be set up. Successful examples include firms such as GE Credit Corporation, several former in-house advertising agencies or consulting firms, repair shops that once only serviced a specific brand, and company educational facilities that are now open to students from outside.

This approach to new product development requires that the initiating company examine carefully its internal resources and ancillary services to determine whether they could perform competitively if made more widely available. (Sometimes, of course, the result of such an analysis may be a decision to contract out the service to another supplier!)

Evaluating New Product "Fit"

The nature of the delivery system for many services means that there is often a high degree of interdependence between existing and new services. As a result, the failure of a new service can also blacken the reputation of existing ones. This is particularly likely to occur when customers are actively involved in the production system, such that the visible portion of the service operations system is large and other customers are encountered during service delivery. For instance, if a hotel introduces services designed to attract a new customer segment, it may not be possible to separate the old and new segments. Incompatibility between the two could discourage both groups from patronizing the hotel in the future. Even if different customer segments do not encounter each other (this would be unlikely in situations where the service firm was trying to develop counter-cyclical business), the new service may not fit well with either the existing facilities or service personnel. Expensive modifications and retraining (or new hiring) may be needed as a result.

Manufacturing firms that enter the service sector often find that they lack the operations and marketing expertise necessary for success in the new context. For instance, existing channels of distribution enable many manufacturers to maintain an arms-length relationship with consumers. Marketing a service may require managing retail outlets and customer contact personnel directly or else getting into franchising. Inventories can no longer be relied upon to balance supply and demand. And quality control is likely to be much more difficult,

Blueprinting Service Design and Delivery

Shostack's (1981) discussion of service blueprinting has already been mentioned. Such a blueprint can quickly become very complex for a service that involves multiple actions taken in sequence with various feasible outcomes. Many service operations, especially those involving numerous company—owned or franchise outlets, codify certain aspects of the blueprint in an operations procedures manual that defines how each task is to be performed. Quality control supervisions acting overtly (or perhaps covertly as "mystery shoppers") then check the performance of service personnel against the criteria laid down in the manual.

The danger with such procedures manuals is that they can be dominated by operational concerns for efficiency that crowd out marketing concerns aimed at satisfying the customer. However, many service firms have essentially redrawn their blueprints to incorporate customer-oriented actions ("make eye-contact with customer, greet customer by name, smile, determine customer need for complementary product and attempt to cross sell, thank customer according to prescribed format" and so forth).

In a very real sense, two sets of blueprints are required for each service. One should describe procedures and systems from the firm's perspective, including what happens behind the scenes. The second should describe the service encounter from the customer's perspective.

Although it may be difficult to test a prototype of a service in its entirety, certain aspects of the blueprint may lend themselves to laboratory testing. Thus mock-ups of a proposed new service facility can be built and tested on prospective customers, employees can rehearse service delivery procedures and problematic customer encounters during training programs, and new services can be test-marketed in limited locations before full commercialization is authorized. The world of entertainment uses dress rehearsals, pre-Broadway "tryouts," and "sneak previews;" banks have evaluated ATM installations in a single branch before going system wide; and Merrill Lynch first test-marketed its Home Equity Account (offering automatic borrowing privileges against customers' net equity in their homes) in California before entering other states with this new service.

The word "blueprinting" has strong architectural and engineering connotations. Yet services are not just processes, they are also frequently human performances. "Screenplay" and "choreography" are two words that may better capture the definition of the human actions within the broader operational blueprint.

Managing the Implementation Process

Although marketing has assumed greater importance in recent years, the operations function still dominates line management in most service institutions. Operations managers are responsible not only for operating equipment and procedures behind the scenes, but also for retail outlets and other facilities used by customers. In labor-intensive services, operations managers direct the work of large numbers of employees, including many who serve the customers directly.

In multi-site service businesses, implementation may take place at numerous local outlets, each of which essentially combines the characteristics of a "factory in the field" and a retail store. It is rare to find marketing managers in the service sector who can exercise line authority at the outlet level. In service organizations with a fairly standardized product line,the best opportunities to exercise control may come from marketing inputs to service manuals that prescribe the standards and procedures to be followed in creating and delivering a new service. However, such an approach is less feasible for customized services.

As service organizations change and adopt a stronger marketing orientation in relation to product enhancement and new product development, there is increased potential for conflict between the marketing and operations functions. As one executive in a service firm commented:

"Marketing's role is typically seen as constantly adding superiority to the product offering so as to enhance its appeal to customers and thereby increase sales. Operations sees its role as paring these elements back to reflect the reality of service constraints - staff, equipment, and so forth - and the accompanying need for cost containment" (Langeard et al. 1981).

Under these circumstances, operations personnel whose performance is measured against cost-related criteria are likely to resist the introduction of new products because they will add to the expenses incurred by their division, branch, or outlet. One approach to dealing with this problem is to decentralize revenue responsibility by transforming cost centers into profit centers. When profit responsibilities are pushed down to the field level, potentially profitable new services take on an appeal they previously lacked for these managers. In a sense, field operations managers find themselves transformed into general managers and become more aware of consumer concerns and of the need for proactive marketing efforts.

There are a number of ways in which service firms are

seeking to reduce the interfunctional stress generated by
development and introduction of new services. One approach is
to transfer managers from one functional department to another
to ensure better understanding of differing perspectives and
also perform an educational role.

A related approach is to create a "task force" to plan
and manage the implementation process. Task forces offer a
way of integrating functional viewpoints into an environment
that is at least partially insulated from the pressures and
distractions of day-to-day management activities. The participants are in a position to create a microcosm of the organization to focus attention on the task at hand, and to discuss and
resolve many of the problems likely to occur during the development and commercialization of an innovative service. There
needs, of course, to be an external mechanism for settling any
disputes which members of the task force cannot resolve among
themselves.

Service innovations must be designed with customer needs
and concerns in mind, requiring a strong orientation toward the
marketplace. But there is also an internal marketplace, in
that innovations usually affect service employees, too. Sometimes innovations involve just minor changes in operating procedures; at other times, they may require major procedural
changes, and retraining or displacement of employees.

Gaining acceptance of service innovations among management
and staff members is a human relations problem. Formation of
a task force is one way of moving the project off the drawing
board and into the development phase - "dimensioning the dream."
But final implementation requires that members of the task force interact with operating personnel in the field. Winning
the acceptance of unit or branch personnel requires that senior
field management sell the project to people at the branch or unit
level. Sometimes this requires field visits and one- on -one
training sessions; at other times, it may be accomplished
through use of sophisticated training films.

CONCLUSION

Service marketers have much to learn from existing knowledge of the new product development process derived from the
study of innovations in manufactured goods. More recent research now offers insights that speak directly to issues distinctive to developing and introducing new services. This paper
offered a number of observations on factors that stimulate new
service development, sources of new service ideas evaluating
how well proposed new services fit the existing operation, blue-

printing and testing the design of new services, and managing the implementation process. One key caveat in all this is not to regard services as homogeneous. Managers should look outside their industries for insights from organizations that have faced (and resolved) similar problems. However, they should recognize that there are limits to the value of generalizations on new service development when it comes to working on highly specific issues.

REFERENCES

Gross, I. (1968), "Toward A General Theory of Product Evolution: A Rejection of the 'Product Like Cycle' Concept," Marketing Science Institute Working Paper, 43-10.

Heany, Donald F. (1983), "Degrees of Product Innovation," Journal of Business Strategy 3; (Spring), 3-14.

Kotler, Philip, William Gregor, and William Rodgers, (1977), "The Marketing Audit Comes of Age," Sloan Management Review (Winter), 35-43.

Langeard, Eric, John E.G. Bateson, Christopher H. Lovelock, and Pierre Eiglier (1981), Services Marketing: New Insights from Consumers and Managers, Cambridge, MA, Marketing Science Institute.

Lovelock, Christopher H. (1984), Services Marketing, Englewood Cliffs, NJ: Prentice Hall.

Shostack, G. Lynn (1981), "How To Design A Service," In J.H. Donnelly and W.R. George, Marketing of Services, Chicago: American Marketing Association.

Urban, Glen L, and John R. Hauser (1980), Design and Marketing of New Products, Englewood Cliffs, NJ: Prentice-Hall.

Wind, Yoram J. (1982), Product Policy: Concepts, Methods, and Strategy, Reading, MA: Addison-Wesley.

PARTICIPANT PERSPECTIVES ON NEW SERVICES DEVELOPMENT SYSTEMS

Facilitators:
C. Robert Clements, University of Massachusetts –
Boston Harbor Campus
Ronald Stiff, University of Baltimore
John A. Czepiel, New York University

In considering new approaches to service development systems, the groups agreed on several observations:

1. The models currently available for product development for goods are applicable to services.
2. The major differences in service development lies after conceptualization in the evaluation and implementation stages due to the need to involve employees servicing customers for the new service in the implementation process.

Christopher Lovelock's suggestion that services marketers start with the existing innovation management models from the goods manufacturing sector generated many responses from the participants. For example, one participant reported the installation of an operations system in a service firm based on Booz, Allen and Hamilton's New Product Development System. In this application, the need was cited to slow down early stages of service development to insure full participation and detailed thought by all relevant parties. A distinction is being made between "service bureaucrats" and "service enthusiasts." The negative criticisms and exclusionary rules of the "service bureaucrat" must be withheld until the full formulation of a service idea/concept by the "enthusiasts."

Another group explored the similarities of the early stages of the New Product Development System model for goods and services -- e.g., setting objectives, generating ideas, etc. However, they felt that potential financial returns were easier to determine for goods and could be done at an earlier stage because of the functions provided by manufacturing engineers. They also felt the need for a more formal screening approach in services to discourage "nifty ideas" and the "product-of-the-month" syndrome.

This second group felt it was in the latter stages of the New Product Development System model, especially the evaluation stage, that major differences occur because of the greater involvment of consumers in the service production process. Thus the services marketer cannot be as divorced from the design

process as the goods marketer. The challenges of test marketing a service were considered -- e.g., how to isolate a market
to test, testing only after operationalization -- this is far
more complex for services.

This group felt that success in services development is
the result of hard work and exacting attention to details, including an analysis of fail points. They concluded that empir-
ical research via actual industry situations is needed to ana-
lyze the types and extent of differences between developing new
services and goods. The Shostack model for blueprinting was
considered to make a contribution to the required detail for
proper implementation planning.

All groups agreed that the Shostack model for blueprinting
to service development was distinct from the Booz, Allen and
Hamilton model. Many of the participants believed it has high
utility for services marketing managers. One group expressed
a concern that the blueprinting procedure had not yet been demonstrated to generate major innovations. The example provided
is a "me too" product having consumer perception differences
only with respect to the specific subset of financial instruments offered, as well as possible quality differences. A fear
was voiced that the application of blueprinting too early in
the true service innovation development process may build in a
rigidity and thus hamper development. This is especially likely to occur if "service bureaucrats" are at the helm.

The focus on characterizing a true service innovation versus an existing service modification was continued by the third
group. They felt the Booz Allen New Product Development System
model was sufficient for service modifications in which the
greatest need for new ideas and approaches exists in the latter
stages of the model. For true service innovations, however,
they felt the beginning stages of ideation, conceptualization
and concept testing were crucial. This led to the observation
that currently most of so-called "new services" were not of the
innovation variety, but instead were improvements internally
initiated from technological advances, excess capacity of assets
and systems, and the like. Competitive adaptation also forces
such improvements. Thus the Shostack model may be core to the
most frequent type of existing new service development activity.

This third group suggested the following sequence for the
services development process:

- Improvements to existing services lead to changes
  in how the customer relates to the service/organ-
  ization.

66

- Then technological capacity may expand functional uses of the service systems and these new functions are truly new services -- not just better ways of doing the same old thing.
- Finally, as consumers start to question fundamental functional assumptions of the system, they begin creating major innovations out of that system.

Thus the service development process is driven by internal forces initiated by the organization itself, rather than as a response to changing customer needs. The group did not feel that this "reverse" sequence was necessarily bad, although it is contrary to the marketing concept.

Innovations of services based on consumer needs via marketing research has not yet been widely utilized by service firms to-date. This may be due to the inherent complexity and the difficulty for consumers to conceptualize such innovations. However, methodology for approaching this type of research effectively would be very useful to service marketers in the future.

NEW SERVICES DEVELOPMENT AND THE EMPLOYEE

Stephen A. Zimney
Senior Vice President
Yankelovich, Skelly and White, Inc.

ABSTRACT

We hear much talk today of the shift in our
society toward a service economy and away from
smokestack industries. And a great deal of this
talk centers about the identification of "what
will be delivered" to the consumer or business end
user. Marketing researchers compile statistics on
the demand for these new "product" categories,
while demographers and other business planners
predict the numbers of people needed to fill the
newly created non-manufacturing jobs of the
future. Still others attempt to outline the
training and re-training needs of millions of
workers in an attempt to build a service centered
economy that will rival, in efficiency, the manu-
facturing-based core of America during the
approximately 20 years that followed World War II.

But, in order to fit employees to the demands
of service jobs, a number of important and fundamental differences must be examined and
understood by those expecting to enter the
marketplace with a competitive edge. Essentially,
these differences can be summarized under four
subject headings; each one to be discussed in
turn:

1) A Changed Environment - a dialectic shift
   in our socio-economic orientation and its
   effect on peoples thinking and priorities.

2) Job Differences - in the service sector
   that can importantly be explained by the
   notion of "Discretionary Effort".

3) Worker Differences - due in large part to shifts in work values.

4) Introducing Change - in a service driven corporate culture which calls for a redefined balance between leadership and management skills.

A Changed Environment

Yankelovich, Skelly and White, Inc. has been gathering data on the social environment for over fifteen years. These investigations have identified major trends in public values , attitudes and lifestyles. These trends are now converging on the world of work, suggesting that the standards we use to evaluate human resource systems are changing in ways that will have dramatic consequences. To appreciate this point it is necessary to provide some historical perspective on the basic shifts in the social climate that have occurred in recent decades.

After World War II, America experienced a period of unparalleled economic growth. The country industrialized rapidly, and American technology, developed due to the necessities of war, became preeminent. Overseas, America was recognized as the world's first superpower, militarily superior to all nations, and the unquestioned leader and defender of the free world. At home, the extraordinary power of the economy fostered a new and broader middle class, which began to emerge during the postwar years. Scores of Americans, by virtue of their increased access to affluence and higher education, began to realize the American dream. Upward mobility and middle class life-styles became the norm, and, by 1950, about 70% of the population was considered middle class.

A Changed Environment

Yankelovich, Skelly and White, Inc. has been gathering data on the social environment for over fifteen years. These investigations have identified major trends in public values, attitudes and lifestyles. These trends are now converging on the world of work, suggesting that the standards we use to evaluate human resource systems are changing in ways that will have dramatic consequences. To appreciate this point it is necessary to provide some historical perspective on the basic shifts in the social climate that have occurred in recent decades.

After World War II, America experienced a period of unparalleled economic growth. The country industrialized rapidly, and American technology, developed due to the necessities of war, became preeminent. Overseas, America was recognized as the world's first superpower, militarily superior to all nations, and the unquestioned leader and defender of the free world. At home, the extraordinary power of the economy fostered a new and broader middle class, which began to emerge during the postwar years. Scores of Americans, by virtue of their increased access to affluence and higher education, began to realize the American dream. Upward mobility and middle class life-styles became the norm, and, by 1950, about 70% of the population was considered middle class.

For most people, classic American values - the Protestant Ethic - set fairly inflexible standards of behavior: the nuclear family - with the husband as sole provider and head of household, and the wife as homemaker and mother - was the accepted norm.

During this period, success was demonstrated by ownership of certain material possessions: a large car, an expensive home, and the latest appliances. There was great optimism about the future as economic vitality continually increased.

70

In fact, by the end of the 1950's, the idea that the nation was capable of nearly unlimited economic growth had become prevalent.

With the rise of this unprecedented optimism came a new social phenomenon: the Psychology of Affluence. In other words, many had come to believe that affluence was no longer something that had to be struggled for, instead, it was considered the logical by-product of America's endlessly expanding economy.

By the end of the 1950's, America's puritan heritage began to assert itself in a new way: instead of self-denial and self-sacrifice, Americans (consciously or unconsciously) moved to fix everything, the perceived economic and social inequities of society were a subject of great concern.

During the 1960's, in response to this new desire for change, corporate ownership was spread over an increased number of stockholders, altering corporate goals and introducing the era of professional management, which paved the way for the growing power of Wall Street.

There was a focus on worker happiness, instead of worker productivity, and an emphasis on business' responsibility to society: if business was unwilling to meet that responsibility, then government would step in to regulate it.

Medical care was seen as inequitable, our commitment to it seemed inadequate by the standards of an affluent society. Both employers and government began to address this gap.

Other social causes were advanced. The Civil Rights movement had begun by this time, and activists continually pointed to the inequities in society as whites achieved economic success while the door was barred to blacks.

A fundamental shift in values underlies all
these developments: the nation's economic strength
changed the population's life goals from
materialism and upward mobility to self-
fulfillment and an emphasis on enjoyment and
experience. The traditional goals and life-styles
of the Protestant Ethic - money, success, rigid
moral standards - were replaced by the New Values
- the focus-on-self, creativity, self-expression,
and freedom from moral and financial constraints.
In other words, the New Values allowed flexibility
in the quality and style of American life while
producing a social agenda based on the assumption
of permanent economic strength.

But by the late 1970's, the assumptions that
had engendered the "fix everything" trend were
weakening.

New economic realities had developed, and both
business and the public began to doubt the idea of
unlimited economic growth. Inflation and
unemployment were painful and seemingly intrac-
table problems.

The massive government spending programs of
the 1960's, designed to "win the war on poverty"
and to end racial discrimination were called into
question as poverty and inequity contined while the
national debt and inflation rose at an alarming
pace.

The population was aging: the postwar baby
boom generation had reached their 30's and were
confronted by an America in which the efforts to
"fix everything" seemed to have created a
situation that itself needed fixing.

In confronting these realities social values
shifted still again, so that by the early 1980's
five new themes have taken shape.

o   First and foremost, our optimism is on the
wane. By 1980, most Americans were conceding that
it was not possible to achieve the hopes of the
previous decades. This "new realism" is evident
across society - workers and managers, consumers,
government officials and political activists.

o   Our tempered optimism carries with it a new
cost-effectiveness orientation. Benefits are now
measured more against costs and less against
abstract ideals.

o   The "psychology of entitlements" has
declined and support for meritocracy has grown.

o   There is a growing commitment to
"strategic" nonideological thinking - to winning -
to entrepreneurship. For example, many consumers
are trying to "beat the system," are bypassing
traditional distribution outlets; indeed, are
bypassing professionals.

o   There has been a rediscovery of the value
of "wit and wisdom." As society has become more
complex and technologized, the need for wit and
wisdom has not been displaced - it has been
enhanced. For example, the growth of specialists
in so many fields has resulted in the resurgence
of generalists.

In summary, if the 1950's were characterized
by self-denial, a future orientation, and a belief
in the power of hard work in a climate of economic
growth, and if the 1960's and 1970's were characterized by a zeal to fix the quality of American
life, and a trend toward focus-on-self, less
rigidness, self-fulfillment, and social responsibility, then the 1980's can be described as a
shift toward adaptation, toward blending social
and economic goals. Americans are attempting -
through ingenious strategic planning, com-
petitiveness, and a greater emphasis on personal
skills and self-reliance - to retain the gains
made by the social agenda of the 1960's. In this
climate almost all assumptions are being re-
examined, including those about work. It is an

appropriate time to stop and take a hard look at the implications for service businesses, emergent out of the 1960's new values thrust:

Job Differences

Within this new environment we must examine the demands of the job and how employees are expected to perform.

If there is one point to make about the changed nature of service jobs it is that with their structure comes a dramatic increase in discretionary effort. Dan Yankelovich, in a recent study of the American work ethic, points to the concept of discretionary effort as heretofore misunderstood and consequently (because it has been mismanaged) has contributed to our lowered productivity. His definition is "...the difference between the maximum amount of effort and care an individual could bring to his or her job, and the minimum amount of effort required to avoid being fired or penalized; in short, the portion of one's effort over which a jobholder has the greatest control.

While it is true that some service jobs are relatively low in discretion, most are high and fall into three broad categories:

.. Point of Sale/Point of Customer Contact Jobs

.. "Backroom" Service Jobs characterized by non-routinized judgments and work order sequencing

.. High Skill/Knowledge Jobs relying heavily on new technologies.

In contrast to low discretion jobs where managements' goal was to put in place a series of very tight procedurial guidelines followed by remedial actions (e.g. quality control inspections) to correct for misplaced discretionary effort when it occurred, the high discretion workplace challenges management to motivate employees to give their discretionary effort in support of the company's goals.

74

The trend continues toward growth of a high discretion workplace, with almost 50% of today's labor force reporting that they have "freedom to decide how they do their work."

Worker Differences

The failure to effectively meet the challenges presented to management today has often been attributed to a fundamental weakening of the work ethic -- a slippage in people's desire to work hard and increase overall productivity. While some work ethic erosion has taken place in a minority of the population, the overwhelming evidence is that the major reason underlying the less than fully motivated workforce points directly to a failure of managers to support and reinforce the work ethic. The work ethic may be asleep for many, but it is not dead.

As noted earlier, the social environment has changed and with it a reduction in the power of "carrot and stick" as primary motivators. Instead, new values workers (high proportions populate service jobs) present new priorities for management to consider as motivational tools. In this connection getting employees on board requires that management understand what is of importance in today's working environment. The following list represents the ten most important job factors as viewed by employees nationwide, reported by Dan Yankelovich in "Putting the Work Ethic to Work",

MOST IMPORTANT JOB VALUES
(out of list of 46 items)

	Who think item very important %
Working with people who treat me with respect.	88
Interesting work.	87
Recognition for good work.	84
Chance to develop skills, abilities, and creativity.	83
Working for people who listen if you have ideas about how to do things better.	83
Having a chance to think for myself rather than just carry out instructions.	83
Seeing the end results of my efforts.	82
Working for efficient managers.	79
A job that is not too easy.	78
Feeling well-informed about what is going on.	78

More importantly it is critical to begin distinguishing between factors which satisfy people (but may have little or no effect on productivity) and those which motivate and directly impact individual commitment to the job. Again from the recent Yankelovich study, the following two charts dramatize the difference.

FACTORS THAT ENHANCE PRODUCTIVENESS

	Would Work Harder For %	Makes Job More Agreeable %	Both %
Good chance for advancement.	48	22	19
Good pay.	45	27	22
Pay tied to performance.	43	31	16
Recognition for good work.	41	34	17
Job enables me to develop abilities.	40	27	21
Challenging job.	38	30	15
Job allows me to think for myself.	37	33	17
A great deal of responsibility.	36	28	14
Interesting work.	36	35	18
Job requires creativity.	35	31	20

FACTORS THAT ENHANCE JOB SATISFACTION

	Makes Job Agreeable %	Would Work Harder For %	Both %
A job without too much rush and stress.	61	15	13
Convenient location.	56	12	12
Workplace free from dirt noise and pollution.	56	12	12
Working with people I like.	54	17	13
Get along well with supervisor.	52	19	12
Being informed about what goes on.	49	21	16
Flexible work pace.	49	21	16
Flexible working hours.	49	18	15
Good fringe benefits.	45	27	18
Fair treatment in workload.	45	24	18

Introducing Change

Finally, we turn to the issue of participation and introducing change to organizations.

The importance of employee participation in linking the needs of employees with the business goals of service organizations has been growing steadily. Employee participation may be considered as a generic process through which organizational systems adapt and adjust to operate more effectively. They do this, in part, by defining and reinforcing the common objectives of employees and management.

As employees and managers explore new ways to work more effectively and meet individual needs on the job, commitment is strengthened. Commitment, both to the job and organization, provides the motivational lever for increasing the level of discretionary effort which employees expend in their jobs. This discretionary effort potential, when raised in a work environment which recognizes its importance and facilitates its development, paves the way for better performance. A frequent and positive concomitant of increased commitment and performance is heightened job satisfaction and morale.

Employee participation, then, is more than a means for enabling employees to enjoy their work more. Participation is a strategic mechanism for allowing employees to become more involved in their jobs, more committed, and more productive. Managed effectively, participation can work to everyone's advantage.

Participation fuels commitment in several ways. On a general level, participation serves to increase employees' sense of ownership once an organization has decided upon a new business strategy, direction, structure, long-term realignment or repositioning. Organizations in transition need cooperation and support at all levels. Employees are more likely to provide this assistance when they feel as if they have an active role in the transition. This tendency, while played out by individuals, is rooted in the fundamentals of human behavior.

Participation further strengthens commitment
by serving as a consensus-building mechanism which
helps to ensure that key groups agree on the legitimacy and wisdom of the transition process.
Agreement increases the probability that employees
will all be pulling in the same direction.

It is important to illustrate the full set of
connections between organizatinal change, consensus building, participation, and commitment.
Figure 1 illustrates the basic stages which organizations go through during a system-wide transition process. The seven stages along the left
margin, from goal setting to acculturation, unfold
most smoothly when commitment levels are high.

FIGURE 1

The Role of Participation In
Organizational Change

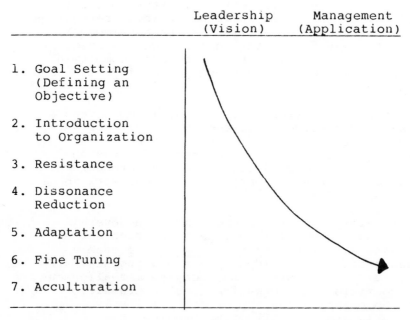

	Leadership (Vision)	Management (Application)
1. Goal Setting (Defining an Objective)		
2. Introduction to Organization		
3. Resistance		
4. Dissonance Reduction		
5. Adaptation		
6. Fine Tuning		
7. Acculturation		
	Inspirational Autocracy	Managed Participation

Commitment to change and visionary leadership set the adaptation process in motion. Goal setting and strategy formulation are top management's responsibility as leaders within the organization. Ultimately, their job is to stimulate commitment among employees as change processes unfold.

It is common for leaders to encounter layers of resistance to change as new programs are introduced within an organization. Overcoming this resistance -- and reducing the dissonance employees feel concerning the rationale for former versus new modes of operation -- is facilitated by delegating managerial responsibility downward. That is, at each successive stage in the change/adaptation process, employees are increasingly called upon to participate in management (as opposed to leadership) roles. The farther an organization moves through the transition process, the more employees actually manage the operational procedures and mechanisms. This progressive, downward transfer of management responsibility (participation) boosts commitment by enabling employees to exert meaningful control over those specific aspects/implications of the change process about which they are most knowledgeable and skillful.

In summation, we have an opportunity to move forward, recognizing the demands being placed on us by the new service economy. The call for leadership in striking a new balance between management authority and employee dignity is fairly clear, while the resistances deriving primarily from American management traditions and, in part, from the human condition remain more obscure as we try to overcome them.

NEW SERVICES DESIGN, DEVELOPMENT AND IMPLEMENTATION AND THE EMPLOYEE

Benjamin Schneider, University of Maryland, College Park
David E.Bowen, University of Southern California, Los Angeles

Abstract

Three critical ways in which products/manufacturing organizations differ from services/service organizations are presented as a basis for designing the "service cube." These differences (intangibility, simultaneous production and consumption, customer participation in production) are used as a framework against which six propositions about employee involvement in the design, development and implementation (ddi) of new services are presented. The propositions specify the benefits that accrue to organizations when employee participation is high, specific facets of new service ddi to which employees are likely to make contributions, and the role of customers as "partial employees" in new services ddi.

The major purpose of the present paper is to explore the role of employees in the design, development and implementation (ddi) of new services. Originally, the focus was to be new service development exclusively, but as that topic was pursued it became clear that design is the first step in the process of bringing new services on line and implementation perhaps the most critical. As will become clear, it appears as if employees in that part of the service sector characterized by high contact with the consumer may be more useful in the development and implementation of services than in their initial design.

It is important to underscore at the outset that this consideration of the employee's role in ddi is framed in a particular context—the service sector, and from a particular vantage point— the literature of organizational behavior. Since the reader of this paper is likely to be more familiar with the marketing and consumer behavior literature on the service sector a brief introduction to the role of the service sector in contemporary organizational behavior (OB) is presented first. Then a definition of service is presented that keys on three characteristics of service and the nature of service organizations. These three characteristics yield the "service cube" which provides a useful way to identify the service employees who are the focus of ddi. Some propositions are then offered regarding the importance of the employee in new service ddi in the service sector.

Introduction: OB, and Service

The organizational dynamics of the rapidly growing service sector have received considerable attention in the organizational behavior literature recently. This attention has typically focused on relatively macro issues with a particular emphasis on the overall organizational design of the service system. Examples include a typology of service organizations (Mills & Marguiles 1980), perspectives on the technology of service operations (Mills & Moberg 1982), the application of a dependent demand approach to service operation planning and control (Snyder, Cox, & Jesse 1982), and the design of professional service organizations (Mills, Hall, Leidecker, & Marguiles 1983). Additionally, Chase (1978) has dealt with ways of buffering core technology of the service system to enhance efficiency and Levitt (1972; 1976) has argued for the "industrialization of service" in service system designs to achieve the same end. These works have helped reverse the tendency to view the principles of organization and management that emerged from the study of manufacturing organizations as central, typical, and applicable to all organizations (Miller and Rice 1967; Shamir 1978).

A number of unique characteristics have been attributed to services and service organizations (SO) by different writers. While their lists may vary somewhat, most would agree to the presence and importance of the following three characteristics (Bowen, 1983):

(1) The Output of Service Organizations is Intangible. Services are intangible or much less tangible than physical goods/products (Levitt, 1980). The typical unavailability of physical evidence for judging the quality of service leads customers to rely upon factors associated with the delivery of the service (employees' dress, manner of speaking, behaving, etc.) in forming their service quality views. Shostack (1977a) notes that because of this intangibility, more than one version of "reality" may be found in a service market. In her words, ". . .the reality of a service varies according to the mind of the beholder. . ." (1977b; p. 42). In a similar vein, Swan and Comb (1976) speak of services as having "expressive performance" (compared to "instrumental performance") and Gronroos (1982) refers to "functional quality" (compared to "technical quality"). What they mean is that in the relative absence of tangibility, the process by which the intangible is delivered becomes the focus for what the service is. In fact, Schneider and his colleagues (Schneider, Parkington & Buxton 1980; Schneider & Bowen 1983) have shown that employee descriptions of how they deliver service is strongly reflected in customer descriptions of the quality of service they receive.

83

(2)   Services are Produced and Consumed Simultaneously.
Whereas with goods there is typically a delay between production
and consumption, with many services production and consumption
occur simultaneously. In services, there typically are no middlemen
or intermediate distribution linkages between production and
consumption.   Consequently, the production function cannot be
divorced from the marketing function (Fitzsimmons & Sullivan 1982)
and the sales force and production team are sometimes one and the
same—particularly in professional service firms (Lovelock 1981).
This characteristic of services yields some unique management
problems, especially the coordination of supply and demand (Sasser
1976; Snyder et al. 1982) due to the impossibility of inventorying
services on the intangible or high customer contact extreme (Chase
1978).

(3)   Customers often Participate in Producing Services. In
many SOs, productivity is in part dependent upon the knowledge,
experience, motivation, behavior, and cooperation of the customer
(Gersuny & Rosengren 1973; Lovelock 1981).   For example, the
reliability of a doctor's diagnosis may depend upon the patient's
ability and willingness to describe his/her illness. Additionally, SOs
having any element of self-service (e.g., automatic teller machines)
require considerable self-discipline and autonomous action from
customers (Eiglier & Langeard 1977).   The SO's ability to manage
customer   behavior   will,   therefore,   be   a   determinant   of
organizational effectiveness.   In other words, managers in SOs can
be thought of as simultaneously managing organizational and
consumer behavior (Bowen 1983).

Especially as the service becomes more high contact and
intangible, SOs are increasingly faced with the management of the
behavior of both employees and consumers. This is true because, at
the boundary of high-contact SOs, employees and consumers are not
only physically close but close psychologically as well.   They are
psychologically close for three reasons: (1) employees of SOs tend to
choose service sector jobs rather than jobs in other sectors because
they   are   service-oriented   and   empathize   with   the   consumer
(Schneider 1980; Schneider & Bowen 1983); (2) consumers complain to
employees at the boundary about service quality; and, (3) service
sector employes tend to be consumers of the same kinds of services
they deliver.

A convenient way to think about the nature of services and
the organizations that deliver them is shown in Figure 1, the "service
cube." The service cube summarizes the three attributes outlined
above (intangibility, simultaneous production and consumption, and
customer participation in the production of the service). In what

84

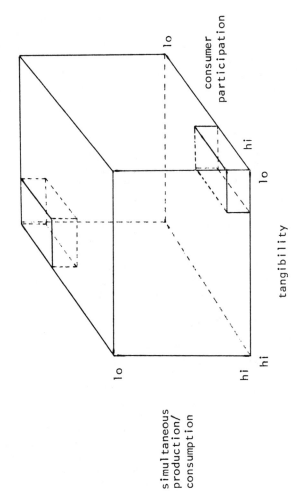

FIGURE 1. THE SERVICE CUBE

simultaneous
production/
consumption

lo

hi

hi

tangibility

lo

hi

consumer
participation

lo

follows, the word service will refer to attributes more toward the bottom right-hand portion of the cube while goods will refer more to the top left-hand portion of the cube. In addition, we will restrict our comments to that portion of the service sector called consumer service organizations rather than to those known as professional service organizations (Fitzsimmons & Sullivan 1982; Sasser Olsen & Wyckoff 1978). Professional service organizations have large numbers of highly educated, highly skilled and highly paid individuals working as doctors, dentists and lawyers. Our focus is more on the fast-food, retailing and banking lower level employees who have high contact with consumers to whom they deliver a relatively intangible service.

While these service employees work in organizations that provide services more tangible than those typically offered by a lawyer or doctor, the fact that they work with people rather than inanimate raw materials makes their job unique from the manufacturing sector. In this context, a most interesting summary view of how SOs generally differ from their manufacturing counterparts can be found in two metaphors from Bell's (1973) book on post-industrial society. Bell described work in the post-industrial world as primarily a "game between persons." In contrast, Bell described work in an industrial society as a ". . .game against fabricated nature, in which men become dwarfed by machines as they turn out goods and things" (1973: pp. XVI, XVII). In what follows, the emphasis is clearly on the game between persons.

Employees and New Services
The organizational behavior literature on employee participation in workplace decisions indicates that participative decision making is superior to authoritarian decision making (i.e., management alone making the decisions) when employees possess important information that management does not (Vroom & Yetton 1973). Also, employee participation in workplace decisions increases their understanding and acceptance of the decision which, in turn, facilitates implementation of those decisions (Locke & Schweiger 1979; Maier 1983). Since service organizations management may understand customer needs less well than employees do and since customers often equate services with the manner in which employees render them, the following proposition is offered:

Proposition 1:   . The more employees are involved in service as defined by the service cube the more important it is to involve them in the ddi of new services.

86

In a recent study by Langeard, Bateson, Lovelock and Eiglier (1982), field managers from two large banking institutions were unable to accurately assess the needs customers, themselves, claimed they had. This example of management being out of "sync" with customers is probably not unique. Proposition 1 follows from a view of service employees as "boundary spanners" with empathy both for the employing organization and the consumers being served. As stated earlier, these employees are both physically and psychologically close to their customers. Because of this, service employees at the boundary of the organization are a source of valuable information about customer needs. In a sense, then, when these boundary employees participate in ddi customers, too, are represented in the ddi process. Thus, particularly in settings of high customer–employee contact, employees are more likely to be aware of the kinds of new services likely to meet customer needs. Perhaps more importantly they are likely to be a source of valuable ideas for how to implement the new service so that customers will respond favorably to change. In this latter perspective on employees, i.e., that they are a source of valuable information to facilitate change, management would involve employees not only to gain their acceptance and commitment but because they are a source of valuable ideas.

Capoor (1981), in reporting on Touche Ross' approach to understanding service businesses clearly promotes this vantage point. He notes that a cycle of people providing service in partnership with customers generates the success that rewards people, and so on. This cycle obviously treats employees (people) as an integral component of service success, especially through their interventions with customers.

A second reason for this proposition builds on the ideas of Swan and Comb (1976) and Gronroos (1982) regarding the principle that as the service becomes more intangible, how the service is delivered is what the service is to the consumer. Gronroos (1982, pp. 5-6) put it thus: In service businesses, "the consumer is not only interested in what he receives as an outcome of the production process, but in the process itself. How he gets the technical outcome-or technical quality-functionally, is also important to him and to his view of the service he has received." Schneider (1980), from a similar vantage point, has proposed that the climate for service created in an organization, including how service is delivered, is critical for service unit effectiveness. In fact he has shown that (a) customers can sense the climate for service in different establishments (indeed, how customers viewed employee morale in these establishments was related to how they viewed service quality) and (b) when consumers feel the service climate is "warm and friendly" their perceptions of service quality are more positive and loyalty to the service unit is enhanced (Schneider, 1973).

In sum, if how employees deliver a service shapes the customer's definition of the service reality, then using participative decision making to make service employees accepting and understanding providers of the new service seems advisable. Thus, while models for employee participation in the manufacturing sector are quite compelling, in the service sector participation would seem to be a requirement. Specification of some of the more subtle ways employee involvement in ddi can facilitate customer acceptance of new services is the foundation for proposition two.

Proposition 2: . Employee involvement in ddi of new services should focus not only on the service, per se, but on the organizational or contextual issues required for supporting delivery of the service to customers.

Given new services are intangible, involve customers, and are simultaneously produced and consumed, it is likely the customers will rely heavily upon the act by which the service is delivered in determining their satisfaction with the service, itself. An important question becomes: What organizational conditions facilitate the act of providing services?

Organizational behaviorists have produced considerable evidence to support the following elements as being important components of work effectiveness:

. Employees must have sufficient aptitudes and attitudes to meet the major demands of their job and/or to learn their new job.
. Reward systems in organizations must be tied to behaviors that are important for organizational effectiveness and which fit the needs of employees.
. The behaviors desired from employees must be made clear through the establishment of goals, through providing necessary training, and through the design of appropriate reward systems.

While the management of organizations know at some abstract level that these factors are important, they seem to lack a clear understanding of how to implement them and thus they are rarely put into practice. This is particularly true of management in the still lightly-studied service sector. We suggest that in the service

88

sector managers turn to those individuals who may be most knowledgeable of these components of work effectiveness—the employees themselves.

For example, some recent experience the authors have had when involving employees in new services ddi has yielded the following suggestions for insuring the infracture necessary for a new service's success:

- The marketing department (the source of ideas for new services in this organization) should work with personnel and computer operations to be sure that the new requirements on people and machinery can be met by the time the new service is rolled out; selection, training, software, and so forth.
- The advertising program for the new service should be developed with employee input because employees are familiar with the day-to-day needs and concerns of customers. This familiarity allows employees to provide input on the ways various kinds of customers are likely to respond to an advertising campaign. Paranthetically it is interesting to note that services advertising campaigns are frequently tested on a small sample of customers whereas testing them on a small sample of employees would (a) provide data from a large sample of customers (because each employee interacts with numerous customers) and (b) gain the acceptance and commitment of employees.
- The performance evaluation system should emphasize the kinds of behaviors on the part of employees the new service requires, and employees need to be reinforced for displaying them. Employees meant by this behaviors such as ensuring customer understanding, revealing interest in customer desires, and so forth, rather than easily countable issues like balancing out at the end of the day.

In summary, the principle behind proposition 2 is that employees know the infrastructure details that have to be attended to in ddi of new services so that the new service has a chance for success.

Proposition 3:   . Involvement of employees in new service ddi should focus more on development and implementation than on design.

This proposition follows from the principle mentioned earlier that participation should capitalize on the expertise of participants. In the case of lower level employees in consumer service organizations it can be assumed that, generally speaking, they will be relatively unaware of the financial and market forces requiring or dictating the essential design of new services. However, once the nature of a new service has been specified, employees can be valuable as aids in development and implementation. That is, given their psychological closeness to customers, employees can be trusted to provide relatively accurate impressions about how customers are likely to respond to different forms of a new service, and they are particularly likely to be valuable in specifying what is needed in order to make the roll-out of a new service a success.

In the latter case, as noted above, employees are able to specify the training needs of employees so the new service can be delivered, the possible reaction of customers to planned advertisements of the new service, ways of adapting computer routines for efficiency in delivering the new service, and possible sequencing of the introduction of the new service to make it acceptable to consumers. A way to summarize the importance of this proposition is to refer to the style and pace of new services: Because employees are the providers, they are likely to be aware of the style of delivery most useful to consumers and the pace of the introduction of the new service.

Much of what has been presented so far has focused on style of service delivery but pace is equally important because it connotes change and change is something people typically resist. People resist change when their perception of the status quo is that it is "ok". When people think their needs are being gratified to an acceptable level, they will resist change.

What management typically fails to consider in introducing change, however, is that its current consumers are relatively satisfied; if they were not they would have taken their business elsewhere. Given this situation, management is taking a risk by introducing a new service because the new procedure is likely to be resisted. In Levitt's (1980, p. 100) words: "The most important thing to know about intangible products is that the customers usually don't know what they're getting until they don't get it."

What Levitt is saying with respect to the issue of change is that customers will become aware of what used to happen only after it no longer happens! The caution is obvious: Any change is a risk in terms of consumer reaction. Fortunately employees are available as a source of input on a pace for implementation that might prove less disruptive and cause less recognition of what was.

Perhaps the best reason for consulting with employees is because it operationalizes a procedure for showing concern for customers. Lovelock and Young (1979), for example, mention seven steps to avoiding insensitivity to customers, 5 of which are relevant here:

1. Develop customer trust
2. Understand customer habits
3. Pretest new procedures and equipment
4. Understand determinants of consumer behavior
5. Teach consumers how to use service innovations

From what has been presented earlier, it becomes clear here that employee involvement in ddi can help make these all happen, i.e., employees can provide management with important information on each of these points.

Proposition 4:   . Involvement of employees in new service ddi will help insure that new services will reflect an "ethic of service" as well as an "ethic of efficiency."

Most new services in organizations are introduced for reasons of efficiency. In other words, the changes are desired by management to facilitate productivity through more efficient (less costly) service delivery. This is the logic behind articles like Levitt's (1972, 1976) classic pieces on the industrialization of service.

Similarly, some writers have recommended sealing employees off from customers so that they will be more efficient (Chase 1978; Levitt 1976) or so they are not coopted by customers (Aldrich & Herker 1977). For example, Chase and Tansik (forthcoming) agree with Danet (1981) that customers are problems for organizations because they disrupt routines, fail to do what they are supposed to do, make unwarranted or exaggerated demands, and so on.

These above positions are contrary to two other principles that appear critical to new service ddi: First, it is important to view service organizations against an "ethic of service" rather than solely against an "ethic of efficiency" (Lefton & Rosengren 1966). To adhere exclusively to an efficiency ethic in new service ddi is to pursue a course more appropriate to manufacturing organizations than to service organizations. It also may be an unacceptable course to customers who frequently rely on how warm and friendly the service atmosphere is as a basis for their attraction to the service (Schneider 1973).

91

Secondly, sealing employees off from customers would deny the service organization an opportunity to learn how customers judge the services they receive against their ethic of service. Simply put, the more the needs and capabilities of customers are addressed during new service ddi, the more likely it is that customers will be attracted to take advantage of what the new service has to offer. The more employees both have contact with customers and are involved in new service ddi, the more likely it is that efficiency goals will not overwhelm the service needs of customers. When the latter happens, efficiency becomes a moot issue.

At Citibank, Matteis (1979, p. 150) reports how this happened:

"In taking our cue from the production management disciplines of manufacturing enterprises - a necessary first step, to be sure - we had tended to blur the difference in what a customer expects from a manufactured product as distinct from a service delivered. In gaining the control needed to achieve production efficiency, we had perforce homogenized the service that we processed. By imposing a kind of product uniformity on our processing, we had sacrificed what is the very essence of a financial transaction service: its uniqueness."

The message in Matteis's report of Citibank's industrialization of service is that for each customer the service s/he receives is a unique experience regardless of how many times the organization must deliver the "same" service to others.

In sum, employee involvement in ddi may protect customer service needs from the productivity and efficiency concerns of the organization. The necessity of achieving this balance is underscored by the following observation by Lovelock & Young (1979, p. 169): "In our experience, attempts to improve productivity in service industries all too often demonstrate lack of sensitivity to consumer needs and concerns."

Proposition 5: . In the ddi of new services, organizations should treat their employees as if they were highly valued customers.

Levitt (1980, p. 102) said that:
" . .a customer is an asset usually more precious than the tangible assets on the balance sheet. Balance

92

sheet assets can generally be bought. There are lots of willing sellers. Customers cannot so easily be bought. Lots of eager sellers are offering them many choices. Moreover, a customer is a double asset. First, the customer is the direct source of cash from the sale and, second, the existence of a solid customer can be used to raise cash from bankers and investors - cash that can be converted into tangible assets."

If customers are so valuable to organizations why do organizations spend so little on retaining them but so much on attracting them? By assuming a perspective that integrates organizational behavior and consumer behavior it becomes clear that the vehicle for retaining customers in the service sector is by focussing on the employees who provide customer services. This perspective suggests the principle that when employees feel they are trusted, understood and deemed important by the organization they will want to treat customers in the same way. By wanting to treat customers appropriately, when asked to participate in ddi of new services, they will.

This proposition has some similarity to a recent insightful proposal by Mills, Chase, and Margulies (1983). They suggested, because of the close relationship between employees and customers in service systems, that management of such systems view productivity as a problem in motivating not only employees but motivating customers, as well. Indeed, they suggested that motivating customers to participate in the production of their own services should be part of an employee's job. Why employees might want to do this and how the service system could foster such employee behavior were not specified by Mills et al. (1983); Proposition 5 constitutes that specification.

In a broad sense, Proposition 5 might be thought of as the Quality of Work Life (QWL) proposition. This is true because QWL programs are introduced by organizations in an attempt to enhance the esteem and personal worth employees experience in their work role. It seems fairly clear that QWL programs have little direct effect on short-term productivity but that they have some substantial indirect long-term impact on unit effectiveness. The difference between the short-term productivity and long-term indirect impact on unit effectiveness concerns the difference between, for example, number of sales per hour and absenteeism or turnover; QWL programs affect the latter but not the former (Schneider, forthcoming). Organizations are not the only ones concerned about turnover. In Schneider's (1980; Schneider et al.

1980) research he has found that customers of banks are concerned about employee turnover. In fact, he found that in some bank branches customers would switch their accounts to branches that employees moved to! This is not an uncommon phenomenon in some service organizations, e.g., hair dressers, retail sales of higher priced clothes, auto mechanics, and so on, but to find it in bank branches was a surprise.

Schneider and Bowen (1983) have recently demonstrated statistically that (a) employee reports on organizational human relations practices are correlated with customer reports of the service quality they receive, and (b) employee reports of their own turnover intentions are correlated with the turnover intentions of the customers they serve. These kinds of data clearly lend support to the idea that when organizations treat their employees as if they are valuable customers, employees will treat their customers in a similar fashion. At least one organization, Marriott, has publicly expressed (in the HBR) its decision to build service quality through the retention of quality employees. Furthermore, it has established human resources policies and procedures to achieve that goal (Hostage 1975). Numerous other organizations with similar philosophies are cited in Peters and Waterman's (1983) recent book on organizational excellence.

A closing thought on the relationship between high quality treatment of employees and new service ddi can be offered. Improved treatment by management of the lower-level employees in contact with customers may, in and of itself, transform an "old" service into a "new" one. That is, improved treatment of employees may result in employees improving their treatment of customers. This would likely be perceived by customers as an entirely new service! Indeed, differentiation in its treatment of employees may be a vehicle by which service management can differentiate its service from comparable services offered by competitors.

Proposition 6: . New service ddi can be facilitated by thinking of customers as "partial employees."

This proposition is the converse of Proposition 5 and builds on the notion that increasing the customer's involvement in the service production process (Lovelock & Young 1979) can be one general approach to new service ddi. For example, when customers use an automated teller machine they are acting as both a consumer and a producer. In their role as service producers, customers can be thought of as "partial employees" of the service organization (Bowen 1983; Mills et al. 1983). The service organization then becomes dependent upon the performance of these partial employees (moreso than their own employees) for the successful implementation of the new service.

An interesting issue for service management then becomes how to manage the performance of customers as partial employees. Unfortunately, there is little prior research that deals with how customer inclinations to participate in producing their own service can be influenced (an exception is the Langeard et al. 1981 study that will be reviewed below). However, a theoretical guide to managing customers is the insight by Mills et al. (1983) and Bowen (1983) that customer performance might be usefully viewed as being dependent on the same issues that affect employee performance: abilities and traits, role perceptions, and motivation. That is, if management can impact these ingredients within customers, they may be better able to shape how well customers perform in the implementation of new services.

Bowen (1983) discussed some management strategies for shaping customer performance. For example, the recent study by Langeard, et al. (1981), identified the traits of customers who were more willing to participate in the service creation process. Participatively-inclined customers were more likely to be younger, male, and more educated, to be impatient, to dislike waiting in line, and to like to play with machines. Thus, organizations may be able to select certain customers who are willing to produce their own service.

It was also noted that if the organization wants customers to act as partial employees, i.e., participate in creating their own service, it must make it clear to customers that it indeed wants them to play that role. For example, McDonald's expects its customers to fill the role of "busser," cleaning their own tables after eating. They make this expectation known with numerous highly visible trash cans and tray racks. Other service organizations, if they are designing and developing new self-service alternatives, must consider how the service setting makes clear to the customer the kind of participation required. If this is not done, customers as partial employees will likely perform poorly in implementing the new service.

Finally, service organizations must manage customers' motivation to be attracted to new services. As service organization management approaches the issue of customer motivation, it should be careful not to repeat the errors made in understanding worker motivation. Management theorists initially assumed that employees were motivated solely by economic needs. Over time, it became clear that employees' work behavior was also directed to other needs, e.g., affiliation and self-actualization. The lesson to be learned is that if new services are being planned that involve customers as partial employees then the new services should attempt to appeal to customer needs other than their economic needs. That is, customers may be motivated to participate in new services that are not only less costly, but also new services that are more challenging, fun, etc.

The summary point is that customers represent a unique pool of partial employees when one considers the topic, "New services design, development and implementation and the employee." Indeed, when the new service is a form of automation, e.g., automated bank tellers, the customer as partial employee becomes the central figure in new service implementation.

Summary

The service sector is now the lead sector in the United States economy. Given this, new service development becomes the very cutting-edge of economic growth. The effective management of employees in new service ddi is a critical factor in how sharp this cutting edge can be.

Unfortunately, most of what we know about managing employees has been learned from studies conducted in industrial organizations. In effect, management models have been relatively unidimensional, developed for organizations whose dynamics center on the production of goods, rather than services.

In this paper, the "service cube" was offered to capture the dimensons along which services and service organizations differ from manufacturing organizations. These dimensions (intangibility, simultaneous production and consumption, and customer participation in the production of the service) frame how service employees should be managed, generally, and what their role should be in new service ddi more specifically.

A number of propositions involving new services ddi and the employee were offered that can be summarized as follows:

. Employee involvement in new services ddi is important for at least two general reasons: (1) Employees, because they are psychologically and physically close to customers, can identify customer needs as new service ddi proceeds. They can guide management's choice of: the kinds of new services offered, the procedures that will facilitate the act of providing these services, and the pace at which new services are introduced. (2) Employee involvement in ddi increases the likelihood that employees will behave knowledgeably and willingly in the implementation of the new service. This is critical, since customers may evaluate the new services on the basis of how employees act in rendering them.

. Employee involvement in new service ddi helps guarantee that the process will not allow the efficiency needs/desires of the organization to overwhelm the service needs of the customer. It appears that an "ethic of efficiency" is often the overly-dominant driving force behind new service ddi.

. Treating employees as highly valued customers may encourage employees to, in turn, treat customers better and actively represent their needs in new services ddi. This proposition is built upon an integration of organizational and consumer behavior — a common set of organizational human resources practices can be reflected in the attitudes and behavior of both employees and customers.

. Customers can be viewed as "partial employees" in the ddi of new services. When new services require self-service of customers, service organizations must try to manage how these partial employees implement the new service. This can be done by managing the traits, role perceptions, and motivation of customers.

These propositions present a picture of the employee involved in new service ddi in partnership with both management and customers. This partnership is a natural outgrowth of the unique characteristics of service organizations. Hopefully, research and practice guided by these propositions will generate creative new service alternatives. More fundamentally, attention to these propositions can further our understanding of how services marketing differs from product marketing, as well as how principals of consumer and organizational behavior developed in the manufacturing sector may need to be ammended when applied to various locations in the service cube.

REFERENCES

Aldrich, H. E., and D. Herker (1977), "Boundary-Spanning Roles and Organizational Structure," Academy of Management Review, 2 (April) 217-230.

Bell, D. (1973). The Coming of Post-Industrial Society: A Venture in Social Forecasting, New York: Basic Books.

Bowen, D. E. (1983), "Managing Employees and Customers in Service Organizations: Some Lessons from Organizational Behavior and Consumer Behavior," unpublished manuscript, University of Southern California.

Capoor, R. (1981), "Strategic Planning-Part II," Restaurant Business, (June), 154-166.

Chase, R. B. (1978), "Where Does the Customer Fit in a Service Operation?", Harvard Business Review, 55 (November-December), 137-142.

_____ and D. A. Tansik (1983), "The Customer Contact Model for Organizational Design," Management Science, 29, 1037-1050.

Danet, B. (1981), "Client-organization interfaces," in Handbook of Organization Design, Vol. 2, P. C. Nystrom and W. H. Starbuck, eds., New York: Oxford University Press.

Eiglier, P. and E. Langeard (1977), "A New Approach to Service Marketing, in Marketing Consumer Services: New Insights, Report 77-115, Boston: Marketing Sciences Institute.

Fitzsimmons, J. A. and T. S. Sullivan (1982), Service Operations Management, New York: McGraw-Hill.

Gersuny, C. and W. R. Rosengren (1973), The Service Society, Cambridge, MA: Shenkman.

Gronroos, C. (1982), "A Service Quality Model and its Management Implications", unpublished paper, Swedish School of Economics and Business Admininstration.

Hostage, G. M. (1975), "Quality Control in a Service Business," Harvard Business Review, 53 (July-August), 98-106.

Langeard, E., J. E. G. Bateson, C. H. Lovelock and P. Eiglier (1981), Services Marketing: New Insights from Consumers and Managers, Report 81-104, Cambridge, MA: Marketing Sciences Institute.

Lefton, M. and W. R. Rosengren (1966), "Organizations and Clients: Lateral and Longitudinal Dimensions," American Sociological Review, 31 (December), 802-810.

Levitt, T. (1972), "Production Line Approach to Services," <u>Harvard Business Review,</u> 50 (September-October), 802-810.

_____ (1976), "The Industrialization of Service," <u>Harvard Business Review,</u> 54 (September-October), 63-74.

_____ (1980), "Marketing Success Through Differentiation-of Anything, <u>Harvard Business Review,</u> 58 (January-February), 83-91.

Locke, E. A. and D. M. Schweiger (1979), "Participation in decision-making: One More Look," in <u>Research in Organizational Behavior, Vol. 1,</u> B. M. Staw, ed., Greenwich, CT: JAI Press.

Lovelock, C. H. (1981), "Why Marketing Management Needs to be Different for Services", in <u>Marketing of Services,</u> J. H. Donnelly and W. R. George, eds., Chicago: American Marketing Association.

_____ and R. F. Young (1979), "Look to Consumers to Increase Productivity," <u>Harvard Business Review,</u> 57 (May-June), 168-178.

Maier, N. R. F. (1983), "Assets and Liabilities in Group Problem Solving: The Need for an Integrative Function," in <u>Perspectives on Behavior in Organizations,</u> J. R. Hackman, E. E. Lawler, III and L. W. Porter, eds., New York: McGraw-Hill.

Matteis, R. J. (1979), "The New Back Office Focuses on Customer Service," <u>Harvard Business Review,</u> 57 (March-April), 146-159.

Miller, E. J. and A. K. Rice (1967), <u>System of Organizations,</u> London: Tavistock.

Mills, P. K., R. B. Chase and N. Margulies (1983), "Motivating the Client/Employee System as a Service Production Strategy," <u>Academy of Management Review,</u> 8 (April), 301-310.

_____, J. L. Hall, J. K. Leidecker and N. Margulies (1983), "Flexiform: A Model for Professional Service Organizations," <u>Academy of Management Review,</u> 8 (April), 301-310.

_____ and N. Margulies (1980), "Toward a Core Typology of Service Organizations", <u>Academy of Management Review,</u> 5 (April), 255-266.

_____ and D. Moberg (1982), "Perspectives on the Technology of Service Operations", Academy of Management Review, 7 (July), 467-478

Peters, T. J. and R. Waterman (1982), In Search of Excellence: Lessons from America's Best Run Companies, New York: Harper and Row.

Sasser, W. (1976), "Match Supply and Demand in Service Industries," Harvard Business Review, 56 (November-December), 133-148.

_____, R. P. Olsen and D. D. Wyckoff (1978), Management of Service Operations, Boston: Allyn & Bacon.

Schneider, B. (1973), "The Perception of Organizational Climate: The Customer's View," Journal of Applied Psychology, 57 (April), 248-256.

_____ (1980), "The Service Organization: Climate is Crucial," Organizational Dynamics, 9 (Autumn), 52-65.

_____ (forthcoming), "Industrial-Organizational Psychology Perspective," in Research on Productivity, A. P. Brief, ed., New York: Praeger.

_____ and D. E. Bowen (1983), "Employee and Customer Perceptions of Service in Banks: Replication and Extension With Implications for Integrating Consumer and Organizational Behavior," Unpublished paper, University of Maryland.

_____, J. J. Parkington and V. M. Buxton (1980), "Employee and Customer Perceptions of Service in Banks," Administrative Science Quarterly, 25 (June), 252-267.

Shostack, G. L. (1977a), "Breaking Free From Product Marketing," Journal of Marketing, 41 (April), 73-80.

_____ (1977b), "Banks Sell Services—Not Things," Bankers Magazine, 32 (January), 40-45.

Snyder, C. A., J. R. Cox and J. Jesse (1982), "Dependent Demand Approach to Service Organization Planning and Control," Academy of Management Review, 7 (July), 455-466.

Swan, J. E. and L. J. Comb (1976), "Product Performance and Consumer Satisfaction: A New Concept," Journal of Marketing, 40 (April), 17-30.

Shamir, B. (1978), "Between Bureaucracy and Hospitality—Some Organizational Characteristics of Hotels," Journal of Management Studies, 15 (August), 285-307.

Vroom, V. R. and P. W. Yetton (1973), Leadership and Decision-Making, Pittsburgh: University of Pittsburgh Press.

PARTICIPANT PERSPECTIVES ON NEW SERVICES
DEVELOPMENT AND THE EMPLOYEE
Facilitators:
Nancy Hansen, University of New Hampshire
Valarie A. Zeithaml, Texas A & M University

This group discussed a series of questions exploring the
role of employees in the process of new services development.
The organizations represented within the group ranged from one
which had no public contact employees involved in the design,
development and implementation of new services to the opposite
end of the continuum where one organization had high levels of
involvement by their public contact personnel. There was group
agreement with a number of the Symposium speakers that employees were most appropriately involved in the development and implementation stages rather than the design stage. It was noted
that middle management personnel as well as top management
should become involved in the change process required to manage
the design or implementation of the new service. They can be
particularly helpful in engaging customer contact personnel in
the process.

A number of observations were made concerning what happens
when employees are to be involved in the process. Ben
Schneider suggests that it does not really matter which employees are selected as long as all employees know that some of
them are being involved and who has been chosen. Those not chosen can contribute through the key ones who are involved.
Choose the group that will have the most information. Also,
the employees should be on the same level to avoid inequities
and strained communication - e.g. do not mix public contact personnel and their supervisors. It is important to provide all
public contact employees with information, answers to customer
inquiries, reasons behind company policies and the like on a
regular and frequent basis so that they can perform effectively.
This will keep them from appearing uninformed to their customers. Finally, the use of scripts for all contact employees was
considered. The group felt it may not be effective with higher
skill level people. Indeed, contact people may need some discretion in handling public contact interactions.

Another problem discussed by this group was how top management will stay informed of fine-tuning changes made by contact employees during implementation which modify the initial
design strategy. It was agreed that such changes are inevit-
able and perhaps even preferable. Yet these tactical decisions

may affect future strategic decisions. Creating task forces
of contact employees in large organizations to provide feedback on implementation is one way to keep top management informed. For small and medium size organizations it may be
realistic for management to directly contact employees and find
out what is happening. An effectively functioning feedback
system may already include data on this problem.

Four factors will determine how successful the above suggestions will be in keeping top management informed of implementation change:

1) How well employees understand the organization's objectives;
2) How prepared is the organization and its employees
   for change and for making changes;
3) How able are top managers to divorce themselves from
   automatic modes and give decision-making power to
   contact personnel;
4) Is the timing of any intervention appropriate to
   achieve a positive leverage for instituting a feedback flow on this matter.

Another question that was discussed concerned how much
time top management should devote to internal marketing. If
the company's top management are not marketing oriented, a signal is given throughout the organization to all employees of
this low priority. The reverse is true when top managers are
marketing oriented. The group felt that top management deter-
mines the willingness of other managers to participate in internal marketing by virtue of their own behaviors -- their participation, support and commitment.

A discussion focused on future factors effecting success
of the corporation in managing change. First, the rapidly
changing environment of services has an equal impact on change
to service jobs. This means that the organization and the
people within it have to be flexible in adapting to change.
This will be especially important for training issues. Second,
technology will continue to take over many more service jobs.
Third, given the turbulence anticipated, it will be important
for the firm to be able to identify and measure employees'
readiness for change. Finally, it will become increasingly
important to view employees as assets.

A discussion evolved about the types of research that managers would like to see conducted about the service employees.
Five suggestions were given. First, managers would like a
method of measuring what is going on in the interaction between the contact personnel and the consumer. Second, what are

103

relevant performance indicators for public contact employees who are not directly involved with units of sale - e.g. public utility meter readers. Third, the measurement and control of quality during the interaction between the contact personnel and the consumers need to be better understood. Fourth, research is needed to determine if new venture teams are still being used and, if not, what has replaced them? Finally, research to determine how a competitor's strategy affects the performance of this firm's employees -- e.g., the effects of Burger King's strategy on McDonald employees.

October 17, 1983

A PRESIDENT'S VIEW OF SERVICES MARKETING

Glendon E. French, President, Health/Care Sector

Thank you--welcome to the Philadelphia area. We're
pleased to make Philadelphia our corporate home. We're de-
lighted to see the AMA focusing on SERVICES Marketing here
today.

Meetings like this one and the other work of your Services Marketing Committee will help a great deal in putting
Services Marketing in the proper perspective. Bill George and
the members of the Committee are certainly to be complimented.

My experience indicates there is a considerable difference in marketing a service just as there is a difference in
managing a service business.

I've had the advantage of being on both sides in general
management positions; for products like prescription pharma-
ceuticals and for services like hospital supply distribution
and ARA. ARA, which is a fascinating subject in itself, will
serve as the basis for most of my comments today.

Let's take a look at services marketing from my point of
view at ARA. As a corporation, we view ourselves as the preeminent services management company which continues to provide
innovative, quality service through an experienced and ded-
icated management team. This has been our guiding credo for
the past 24 years and has led us to grow from $20 million to
over $3 billion in annual revenues.

From the very outset, it was clear in terms of long-range
strategic planning that we were in the service business even
though initially we were in only one small segment of it.

It was also clear that if we were to grow we would have
to broaden our service offerings and move into other carefully
selected areas that met some very basic criteria.

Our initial success was based on the fact that we developed a system for providing a service, a direct service to
people.

The demand was constant. The service we provided could
not be postponed, inventoried or imported. And the need would
be greater in the future.

This led quickly to some basic conclusions about our service business--the expertise was transferable. Procedures and systems which proved to be very effective in one business, quite often could be used in another--each business, however, no matter how large or small, represented a unique challenge. No two were really identical. Each demanded specialized solutions, each provided a unique service, and still do.

Today, we have 24 strategic business units which are categorized into six operating sectors managing a wide variety of services, including health and family care, transportation, food, textile rental, maintenance, magazine and book distribution and laundry services.

As ARA's CEO, Joe Neubauer has established five principles to provide our management direction. We don't view them as catchy phrases or mere slogans. I believe they form the very basis of our business and for the purpose of your seminar I'd like to share them with you...

1. To build our business on demonstrably better services than those offered by our competition. And to maintain or establish leadership positions in each major business area or geographic area in which we choose to compete.

2. To deal with integrity, fairness, and responsibility toward all our constituencies and in all areas of business conduct.

3. To ensure that our corporation and each of its operating entities has in place an experienced management team superior to our competition.

4. To assure future long-term growth in profitability and productivity through investment and innovation.

5. To achieve an outstanding financial record through steady, reliable growth and high returns.

These principles are the tools to help us achieve our fundamental business objective which, simply stated, is to develop and retain clients and customers for the services we manage.

Marketing is the key to achieving this objective. A company's future depends on its marketing performance. Everything else in business is a cost, only marketing produces income. Marketing in ARA is not just a set of business functions nor is it another term for "selling." It is a business state of mind (a marketing mentality) which requires all

106

of us to <u>think first of the user of the service</u> and only <u>then</u> of the producer. This applies to both present and prospective clients. A marketing point of view should transcend all our business operations. For if we are always able to provide services for which there are real needs, our clients', customers', shareholders' and employees' interests will all be properly served. Marketing at ARA, in effect, is not a function. It's a philosophy.

Some examples of our principles in action would be the development of innovative approaches which separate us from other organizations.

This list would include:

. the development of a computerized food production system which allows our food service directors to spend more time with the customer and less with the calculator.

. the design of "family reading centers" in supermarkets which expands the store's more profitable non-food sales...and our own.

. the creation of an entire new service we call "Fleet Maintenance Services" to manage and maintain the vehicles for municipal governments and generate real savings for the taxpayer.

In organizing our marketing effort, we believe the marketing specialist support function belongs primarily at the business unit or sector level rather than at the corporate level.

In a product company it's different. The marketing function can be carried out separately by a separate marketing group. In a service organization the marketing functions are really the responsibilities of the operating management. Let me give you some examples of why the differences between services and product marketing require a different approach at ARA:

1. Definition

In a product, the unit is well-defined. Very precise engineering and manufacturing specifications can be developed. As a result, the customer's expectations are well-articulated.

107

In a service, e.g., child care, the unit is not well
defined. The parent's specification is generally
"care for my child." (The best possible care at the
lowest possible cost.) But what is the best care?

2. Ability to Measure

A product can be measured objectively against the
well-ordered specifications--check the tolerances,
compare the weight, color, shape, style, etc.

Measuring a service, e.g., office building maintenance service, is usually subjective when comparing
one service with another. What is clean?

3. Key Process

Once the need is defined, the key to creating the
product response is in the manufacturing process.

In services marketing the "product" really isn't
created until the service is performed. We call this
"service delivery." E.G., uniform rental services,
delivery occurs when the employee puts on the
garment.

Does it fit, is it clean, has it been repaired, was
it available on time? This is obviously quite different from manufacturing a uniform.

4. Distribution Channels

With a product, there is no channel until after a
product is manufactured, packaged, priced and shipped.

In a service, e.g., management of a hospital emergen-
cy room, the channel of distribution is the same as
the delivery of service. A physician treating a
patient is, at one time, manufacturing and distri-
buting his "product."

5. Flexibility of the Service Provider

With a product, the manufacturer is limited to his
tools, dyes and fixtures. Very little change can be
made without substantial time and money costs.

In a service business, the provider has much broader
limits in altering the "product." With a greater
labor intensity as opposed to capital equipment, the
service organization, e.g., magazine and book distribution, can change the types of publications, the
number of books, and the display arrangement relatively easily.

6. Time Interval

In developing products, there is a long period required for engineering drawings, model building, product testing, final production runs, inventory build-
up, delivery through channels and customer feedback.

In a service, e.g., food service management, a manager
in almost the same day goes through the entire life
cycle of a product--menu planning, purchasing, receiving, quality control, production, service, customer
feedback and final accounting.

Because of these differences, we require our line management to develop the "marketing mentality I referred to earlier.

To support this effort we have encouraged our business
unit or sector (group) management to add marketing specialists
at their level. I believe the marketing specialist belongs as
close to the "firing line" as possible in our business. It's
at this level where we have the most specific definition of
marketing:

1. discipline of analyzing client and customer needs
2. design of services and systems to meet those needs
   profitably
3. development of selling methods to activate demand.

At the corporate level, we do have a small group to address those issues which the business units/sectors cannot. At
ARA these include two important programs:

1. the cross-selling of our services by exchanging introductions of additional services to present clients
2. coordinating efforts of client satisfaction and
   quality assurance through third-party surveys

Regarding the development of new services, let me get
back to our key growth strategy which is internal growth. We
have enormous opportunities in our existing markets in all
geographic areas and with most clients. If we are willing to

innovate and adapt, we can grow profitably. We look for productivity improvements in doing things differently, in seeing
what our competitors are doing, in listening to the clients.

The CEO's role is critical here. He must communicate the
importance of an innovative mode. The signal must be clear as
it is transmitted through the organization.

Since every one of our markets is changing every day, the
CEO must encourage managers to be "advocates of change" to
maintain a market leadership position.

We want to make sure of two things:

1. We want to maximize opportunity, not just minimize
    risks.
2. We must recognize there has to be a top line before
    there's a bottom line.

One question I often hear is: How do you measure your
managers' performance off the balance sheet?

I'm pleased to answer that as part of our Annual Business
Plan and Three-Year Strategic Plan, we have developed a format
for measuring "non-financial objectives."

The non-financial objectives included in our Management
Incentive Bonus are not part of the Return On Net Assets or
Earnings Before Income Tax calculations.

The non-financial objectives would include community service, quality assurance, human resource development and
account retention.

Looking to the future, there is great promise for the
business of service management. More and more companies and
institutions forced to cope with increasing economic pressures
are re-examining some of the services they provide themselves
with the view to determining what can be contracted to professional managers. These same economic forces have driven many
local and even state governments to the brink of bankruptcy.

More and more private and public sector organizations will
be forced to the conclusion that they must find a better way,
that they must reduce costs by contracting the responsibility
for certain services to professional managers who will have to
deliver more efficiently, or be replaced. That presents almost
unlimited opportunity.

One dramatic example of that kind of opportunity represents one of our company's biggest challenges in 1984.

We will be managing the food service and the transportation service for all 12,000 of the world's athletes at the Olympic Games in Los Angeles next summer. In addition, we are consulting with the Yugoslavian Government on the food services for the Winter Games there in February.

We call it the "Olympic Challenge."

Think about Los Angeles, for example: 12,000 athletes from 151 countries using 500 buses going to 60 different sites scattered over 2,200 square miles—and consuming over a million meals in just a 15-day period.

We think it's a fair test of our capabilities!

We're confident because we have had experience in nine other Olympic-related events dating back to the 1968 Summer Games in Mexico City.

The only thing we can't figure out is how to handle all the ticket requests we're receiving.

To enable us to evaluate the opportunities of the future, we need better information on services management and productivity.

The current industrial code used by the Commerce Department is strongly skewed in favor of the goods-producing sector. In fact, the 1980 edition of the U.S. Industrial Outlook devoted only eight percent of its space to the services. And then, all services were excluded from its projections beyond the current year, while manufacturing was projected over three years.

Industry, our universities and government need to keep better track and develop more appropriate mechanisms to monitor the production and distribution of services and thereby create more knowledge and understanding of the role of services in our economy.

This is why ARA has established "The Fishman/Davidson Center for the Study of the Service Sector" at the University of Pennsylvania's Wharton School of Business.

We're hopeful it will just be the beginning of other efforts to give the service business the recognition and research it deserves.

We've reviewed ARA's corporate objectives and my views on marketing and our business strategy, and I've enjoyed the opportunity to be with you--and now I'll try to answer any of your questions.